Surviving the Cross

Surviving the Cross

An Evidentialist Appraisal of the Swoon Theory

CHRISTOPHER D. BANKS
with JOHN S. KNOX

Foreword by Israel P. Loken
Afterword by Joe Parle

RESOURCE *Publications* · Eugene, Oregon

SURVIVING THE CROSS
An Evidentialist Appraisal of the Swoon Theory

Resource Publications
An Imprint of Wipf and Stock Publishers
199 W. 8th Ave., Suite 3
Eugene, OR 97401

www.wipfandstock.com

PAPERBACK ISBN: 979-8-3852-1566-9
HARDCOVER ISBN: 979-8-3852-1567-6
EBOOK ISBN: 979-8-3852-1568-3

VERSION NUMBER 010725

Blessed be the God and Father of our Lord Jesus Christ! According to his great mercy, he has caused us to be born again to a living hope through the resurrection of Jesus Christ from the dead, to an inheritance that is imperishable, undefiled, and unfading, kept in heaven for you, who by God's power are being guarded through faith for a salvation ready to be revealed in the last time (1 Pet 1: 3–5 ESV).

Contents

Foreword by Israel P. Loken | ix
Preface | xi
Acknowledgments | xiii

1 Introduction | 1

2 Methodology and Historiography | 8

3 Survey of Literature | 13

4 Apologetical Appraisal | 33

5 Evidentialist Appraisal | 53

6 Conclusion | 73

Afterword by Joe Parle | 79
Bibliography | 81
Subject Index | 85

Foreword

I DISTINCTLY REMEMBER THE day that I first met Christopher Banks. It was the winter of 2019. Christopher arrived at class a few minutes late and took his seat in the last row. I must confess that (in my mind) I immediately wrote him off as a typical student who would probably fail to finish his degree. After class, Christopher approached me and explained that he had been forced to work late. He then surprised me by asking me several penetrating questions about my lecture. I quickly realized that Christopher was a student to keep an eye on.

Later, after Christopher asked me to write the foreword for this book, I went back and reviewed my extensive communications with him. Over the years, he has questioned me concerning a wide variety of topics, including fasting, tithing, wearing head coverings, the Apocrypha, the author of Hebrews, the identity of Babylon in Revelation, whether there are animals in heaven, and what happens to babies when they die. It is clear to see that Christopher has an extremely inquisitive mind.

Thus, it came as no surprise to me when he informed me that he was going to continue his education (in pursuit of a master's degree). What did surprise me was that he volunteered to read and grade papers for my school during his graduate studies. Despite my hasty rush to judgment many years ago, Christopher has become one of the most remarkable students that I have ever had the privilege of teaching and mentoring.

I have read the manuscript for *Surviving the Cross* three times. I have found the content to be fascinating. Following the issue of creation—coupled with the existence of God, the atonement is the second most important topic in apologetics. One might ask why the atonement so important. Simply put, the atonement accomplishes the salvation of those who believe, thus overcoming the catastrophic effects of the Fall. As the Apostle Paul states, "For I delivered to you as of first importance what I also received: that Christ died for our sins, in accordance with the Scriptures, that he was buried, that he was raised on the third day" (1 Cor 15:3–4a ESV).

Without the atonement, there is no resurrection. Without the resurrection, there is no hope for humanity. Our preaching is in vain, our faith is futile, and we remain in our sins (1 Cor 15:14–17). Unfortunately, there are many who deny the atonement. While people typically associate those who deny the atonement with those who either deny the existence of Jesus or with those who believe he was merely human, there are many who deny that Jesus actually died as a result of the cross.

This book provides a conclusive answer to those in the latter category. Moreover, I have found Christopher to be an outstanding apologist. To wit, I encourage everyone to read this book—not only to grow in the faith, but also to become better equipped to answer those who question one's faith. After all, those are the two primary goals of the field of apologetics.

Israel P. Loken, Ph.D.
Chair of Bible and Theology
The Bible Seminary
Author of *The Old Testament Historical Books: An Introduction*
and *The Old Testament Prophetical Books: An Introduction*

Preface

I WAS ON THE hunt for an argument, scrolling through various debates on YouTube featuring Christian apologists and their opponents. That was when I stumbled upon a particularly intriguing debate between Ahmed Deedat and Robert Douglas. As I attentively absorbed both sides of the argument, I felt a growing sense of responsibility. The arguments presented in that discussion ignited a passionate desire within me—a desire to equip fellow Christians for similar debates and challenges. This task resonated deeply with me due to the influences in my life.

Thus, I embarked on a journey to delve into the ideas discussed in that debate, particularly focusing on what is known as the Swoon Theory. To my surprise, I discovered that other scholars had addressed the ideologies of the Swoon Theories, but there was a noticeable absence of theoretical data from a medical perspective.

While the events surrounding the crucifixion and the related historical documents are ancient, some common knowledge exists about trauma, blood loss, and asphyxiation. It was then that I made it my mission to examine the crucifixion from a medical standpoint. I felt compelled to demonstrate that survival following a Roman crucifixion was virtually impossible. The stakes were high because this debate had profound implications for Christianity. As I explain in this book, if the crucifixion were to be proven false, if Jesus did not die on the cross, then the entire foundation of Christianity—from its principles to its doctrines—would lose its meaning. Jesus stands as the cornerstone of truth for Christianity, but without the crucifixion, he would be relegated to the status of a false prophet.

Moreover, the deeply held worldview of many Christians would crumble from despair if the crucifixion were called into question. Hence, the research presented in this book is a culmination of my desire to share the Gospel and provide reasoned explanations for my faith and hope. As 1 Peter 3:15 (ESV) instructs, "But in your hearts honor Christ the Lord as holy, always being prepared to make a defense to anyone who asks you for a reason for the hope that is in you; yet do it with gentleness and respect."

Acknowledgments

LOVE CONSTRAINS ME TO acknowledge those who have a direct hand in this book. First is God. Without God, nothing is possible, and with God, all things are possible (Mark 10:27).

Saskia, my wife, thank you for being a woman of tremendous godly vision who saw this when I did not. Your confidence in me exceeds my expectations of myself. Without your belief, encouragement, and support, I never would have thought to do this. You prove what the love of God accomplishes. I am grateful to God for bringing us together as a witness of His love for all.

To our sons and daughters, Tyron, Christopher Jr., Isaiah, Samuel, Brianna, and even little Abigail, your inquiries on my progress and well-wishing along the way kept me on track. To my mother and father, Jacquetta and Wilbert, thank you for listening to me as I discussed thoughts, providing feedback, and praying for me as I tirelessly worked on this research.

Dr. John S. Knox, your words have always been a source of encouragement and a trustworthy beacon pointing the way forward. Every interaction with you has edified me. You are my editor and mentor, for which I could not ask for a better friend. I would also like to acknowledge Dr. Israel Loken. Through your tutelage, I have learned so much about Scripture and developed a respect for theology. I also acknowledge Alex Hernandez, my first professor, whom I clung to as a child. His love of sharing the Gospel and love for others has helped me in some of my lowest points.

Finally, I acknowledge present and future worshippers whom I have never met. You are partakers of a heavenly calling, and God has planted you as the desire of my heart (Ps 37:4). I pray for your faithful service in love as we consider the faithful example of the apostle and high priest Jesus Christ, our Lord and Savior (Heb 3:1–6).

1

Introduction

FEW PEOPLE'S LIVES HAVE been as influential or transformative as Jesus of Nazareth—the long awaited Jewish Messiah, the Son of God, the perfect Priest and sacrifice, the Savior of the world, and the superlative model of love, obedience, and sacrifice in the Christian religion. Jesus's unexpected arrival and later epoch-making engagement with Judaism in ancient Jerusalem and Judea in the first century CE forever changed believers' understanding of Yahweh and their relationship to the Most High God. Many Christians acknowledge that without Christ's sacrificial death for the sins of humanity (past, present, and future), it is impossible for anyone to reconcile with the Father. Therefore, Christianity ultimately hinges upon the reality the crucifixion and resurrection of Jesus.

In 1 Corinthians 15:14,[1] the apostle Paul suggested that if Christ had not been raised, then what had been preached and what had been believed was undoubtedly false. If so, the very foundation of Christianity is worthless and vain. Not surprisingly, the life and significance of Jesus has (therefore) been internationally

1. All scriptures are taken from the *THE HOLY BIBLE, ENGLISH STANDARD VERSION (ESV)*: Scriptures taken from *THE HOLY BIBLE, ENGLISH STANDARD VERSION* ® Copyright© 2001 by Crossway, a publishing ministry of Good News Publishers. Used by permission.

scrutinized by innumerable Christian, Jewish, Muslim, and secular scholars throughout the centuries. Thus, Jesus is one of the most investigated and discussed persons in history, with countless theories being proffered about his natural and/or supernatural existence, mission, and meaning.

In search of fairness and balanced research for this book, an attempt has been made to accurately reflect mainstream theories of what each party believes to be true regarding Jesus's life, death, and resurrection. Therefore, when a Muslim scholar or religious leader discusses Jesus in this book, it reflects what they believe to be true, per their cultural upbringing and theological presuppositions. For instance, according to Muslim belief, Jesus was merely a prophet of God who did the will of God.

Furthermore, Muslim doctrine asserts that Jesus was a devoted believer and that he was never crucified; instead, he was saved from that extremely painful demise. This is, of course, contrary to the long-held, historically honored tenets of the Christian faith. To further their position on this quintessential matter (and to prove that the Quran is not so far off in its assessment), Muslim apologist Ahmed Deedat and author of *Crucifixion or Cruci-Fiction?* suggests that Jesus Christ never actually died on the cross.

Deedat goes on to say that after Jesus was taken down from the cross, he hid in the tombs to recover from the terrible ordeal he had just gone through. Specifically, his opinion is that being on the cross is a traumatic experience, and Jesus was on the verge of death; however, since the Roman soldier stabbed Jesus, it revitalized him, causing Jesus to remain alive so he could meet with the disciples and prove that death could not hold him.[2]

Deedat bases his rationale on the Lukan account, the reactions of Jesus's disciples, and Deuteronomy 18:20. He also mentions the surprise of the Romans. They were under the impression that Jesus was already dead. The disciples acted as if they saw a ghost, so Jesus, seeking to ease the minds of his devoted followers, ate with them.

---

2. Deedat, *Crucifixion or Cruci-Fiction*, 59–63.

Deedat is not the only individual who believes that Jesus survived the cross. Other well-established Muslim scholars have also argued from the Apparent Death Theory, a.k.a, the Swoon Theory, to detail what happened to Jesus. In affirmation and promotion of this theory, Deedat states that Jesus did not meet his end on the cross. Although the Swoon Theory has been contended by many other scholars,[3] the idea still is being promulgated to persuade others that the Gospels' account of Jesus's death were false.

As previously mentioned, the cross and resurrection of Jesus are vital for the biblical foundations of Christian doctrine and beliefs. Christians have historically promoted the Bible as God's Word, and the Bible is inerrant. Muslims and Christians agree that God cannot lie; however, if the Bible contains false evidence, then its contents can be ignored or discarded.

The Four Gospels all contain the acts of Jesus, the Son of God, but if it is proven that Jesus did not die on the cross and never was resurrected, then all that Jesus stated becomes questionable—including what Christianity believes to be the word of God. Furthermore, according to John 17:21, Jesus and the Father are one. So, if the crucifixion and Resurrection were false, then so might the existence of God (known as Yahweh in the Old and New Testaments) also be false.

For instance, Deedat also argues in *Is The Bible God's Word* that Mark 16:9–20, which discusses Jesus's ascension, was added later; however, he never stated by whom or when it was added. Obviously, his goal is to cause disbelief in the veracity of the Scriptures. Furthermore, Deedat has stated that Mark 16:9–20 is not Scripture nor critical to the Christian doctrine.[4]

Other countless arguments have been brought against the existence and identity of God, the deity of Christ, and the core Gospel message. Christians need to safeguard the faith that gives them joy and salvation (as 1 Pet 3:15 states). Many of the accusations against Jesus and Christianity are nothing new or innovative; instead, they are just remakes of previous arguments, which have

3. Khouri, "Crucifixion in the Qur'an," 158–74.
4. Deedat, *Is the Bible God's Word*, 19.

been debunked and dismissed through hermeneutical and logical analysis.

There are several presumptions that supporters of the Swoon Theory and other Muslim scholars bring to this discussion. From one point, they argue that the resurrected body, based on what Jesus said in the Gospel of Matthew, should be like the angels. If humans are like the angels, flesh and blood cannot inherit or enter heaven, and Jesus had a resurrected body, how could Jesus eat? Is the resurrected body like the physical body, filled with bone, muscles, and tendons? If the answer is no, then what was the significance of touching the body? If the physical body is similar to the resurrected body, then all that theology tells us about the angels and celestial bodies comes into question.

The entirety of their argument warrants a rebuttal from Christian theists; however, instead of debating theology, it would be more prudent to discuss the circumstantial evidence surrounding Jesus's crucifixion because there lies the problem. The problem stems from whether or not Jesus survived the cross—because if Jesus did, then all that Christianity holds dear, the Great Commission and any hope for eternal life, would be false. It would essentially hold no power.

Christians recognize that it was through the crucifixion and resurrection of Jesus Christ that allowed the world was saved; furthermore, it also means that humanity had a personal connection to God through His Son. With this connection, man was able to go to the Father through the Son and be seen, even though man is not worthy of such a thing. It is the Son who cleanses those who follow him so that they can be citizens of God's kingdom. However, without the crucifixion and resurrection, there would be no discipleship, no cleansing, and no amount of prayer that could ever save the world from sin.

From the apologetic side, one of the key points to consider is all the pertinent data at seekers' disposal essentially provides a more precise answer. Looking at the crucifixion from a medical perspective educates readers on what Jesus went through, medically, at that time and also point to an understanding of plausibility of Jesus surviving such an ordeal.

On the question of whether Jesus have survived the crucifixion, from a religious standpoint, it would be difficult to agree with our Muslim scholars about this matter. Some worldviews and points of theology are difficult to overcome, as will be shown as the research unfolds in this book. However, from an area of apologetic evidential argument, it is the goal of this study to share critical and objective information concerning the crucifixion.

Diverging from Deedat's assertions, this book defends the core belief that Jesus died on the cross, and the cause could be linked to not just one medical theory. Following all the scientific evidence substantiated in the Gospel accounts of the Crucifixion, it should be considered that multiple medical factors contributed to and were associated with Jesus's death. The Scriptures (and other historical, extra-biblical accounts) suggest that Jesus, in fact, did die on the cross—thus proving that God's miracle of restoration was at hand, and that Jesus had to die to fulfill the prophecy.

Furthermore, because of the events that happened before and during the entirety of the crucifixion, it can be reasonably proven that survival after the crucifixion was impossible, irrational, and is in denial of proven medical realities. When Deedat talks about the resurrected body and how the crucifixion of Jesus was handled (and the fact that Jesus did not have any broken bones), it is a normal—but unevidential—response for those seeking to dismantle the crucifixion of Jesus. While this could be a hermeneutical problem, this study is geared to provide medical evidence to defend against this type of argument—thus signifying the crucial position on the problem at hand that conclusively affirms that Jesus did actually die on the cross and was factually resurrected, just as the Scriptures state.

There are several myths concerning the crucifixion and resurrection of Jesus Christ. Many of the problems concerning this topic stem from the disbelief in the deity of Christ, from Arianistic assumptions, as well as other doubts regarding the miraculous event surrounding and perpetated by Jewish leaders in the first century CE. Despite corroborating archaeological and historical evidence, many other people (from Jesus's time until today) have sought to prove that the biblical account is incorrect.

From the Christian theist perspective, Jesus is Lord and Savior who came into this world to save all who would believe in him. For most Muslim believers, Jesus is only a prophet—nothing more, nothing less. Yet, John 3:16 states that God so loved the world that he gave his only Son. The implications of this are that everyone who would hear, accept, and follow Christ, they will be saved through the love of God and the redeeming work of Christ. So, it is not just Israel who would be saved, but gentiles alike. However, if Jesus were lying about who he is, then this would not just affect Christians; instead, it would be detrimental to the entire world. Therefore, this book's assertions could possibly bridge the gap between the Christian and Muslim communities with the information presented in this study.

New Testament scholars like Bart Erhman had discounted or found some discrepancies with the Gospels, such as the time when Jesus was taken in the garden. Erhman has affirmed that the Gospels tell one important story—the crucifixion. Yet, according to Erhman, all have important differences in what they tell, as in Mark and Luke.[5] However, Erhman still believes that the historical Jesus was more than likely crucified despite his reservations concerning Scripture (and the resurrection).

With the aforementioned in mind, this book will provide readers with a plethora of data to uphold traditional Christian beliefs about the crucifixion and resurrection of Jesus Christ. Chapter two will explain the methology and historiography employed in this study to preserve scientific integrity of the Gospel resurrection account. Chapter three will include reports from Muslim authors, Jewish documentation, Christian theists, and non-religious groups who will share medical information about this matter. Chapter four examines previous apologetical arguments that may have neglected to add the medical implications of what happens during a typical crucifixion to strengthen the argument. Chapter

5. Ehrman, *Jesus, Interrupted*, 72.

five more fully presents the data uncovered in research, focusing on the Gospel of Luke, the circumstances for the Roman death penalty, and the medical evaluation of what transpires during a typical crucifixion (as recorded in the gospels). The final chapter brings to full circle what the book topic suggests, that there is a multi-causality of medical events that could have contributed to the death of Jesus, and not just one singular position alone.

This book is primarily focused on any and all available evidence regarding the crucifixion. In the realm of evidential apologetics, by evaluating the historical data—piece by piece—that truth will be uncovered. Evidential apologetics tends to focus chiefly on the legitimacy of accumulating various historical evidences for the truth of Christianity.[6] It is through this form of study that serious seekers view the historical findings they wish to share with others regarding the truth of Christianity.

Far from just a superstitious tale from long ago, this study points to numerous scholarly queries from all sides of the debate, thus showing the seriousness of this topic and its scientific scrutiny. Ultimately, this book will argue that by observing all the medical occurrences requisite for a crucifixion (along with proven historical documents), it can be found that there was a multi-causality of medical events that contributed to the death of Jesus—thus furthering the truth that Jesus actually died on the cross. This essential matter—that Jesus physically died on the cross—is also beneficial for the entire world and not just for those of the Christian faith.

---

6. Habermas, "Evidential Apologetics," 92.

2

Methodology and Historiography

THE ONGOING DISCUSSION ABOUT Jesus Christ and the cross has long been a topic between Muslims and Christians alike. Therefore, this study was undertaken to answer the question on whether a man is able to survive a brutal Roman crucifixion. If the answer is yes, then the likelihood of Jesus surviving the cross increases; however, if the results produce a negative response, then the likelihood of survival is not present. Upon answering this question, the following investigation is whether or not it was medically possible for Jesus to survive the crucifixion. Both questions were addressed throughout this body of work.

DATA COLLECTION

Roman antiquity and medical examination were utilized to determine the nature and effectiveness of a Roman crucifixion. Although it was discovered that the Romans did not create the Crucifixion, it was determined that they improved upon its effectiveness. Although the studies from Roman antiquity and the medical examinations do not particularly key into all the factors of Jesus's crucifixion, the reason behind seeking data from these two areas was to ascertain the nature of a typical crucifixion. If there were a chance of survival, what would be the long-term effects of going through that ordeal? Several pre-specified criteria were not used to identify key studies to answer the question.

These areas were: (1) the studies from non-peer-reviewers; (2) none of the studies included recent volunteers to undergo a crucifixion; (3) notes from study Bibles; (4) psychological evaluations from individuals on death row; (5) non-translated Greek, Hebrew, and Arabic documents were not included due to limitations on the researcher.

This research affects all members who call Jesus Christ their Lord, the Muslim party who remains firm in their understanding of Jesus, and those who are seeking the truth of Jesus of Nazareth. Primary sources of this research included works from but were not limited to historians such as Gary Habermas, medical researcher Frederick Zugibe, and Muslim apologist Zafar Harris.

Procedures Used

By utilizing Google scholar and other library resources, several keywords were used. Words like crucifixion, Roman execution techniques, Roman antiquity, asphyxiation, blunt force trauma, forensic crucifixion, heart attack, hematohidrosis, bloody sweat, blood, and water these results produced the medical data found to produce the findings in this study. Furthermore, this search also focused on what was agreed upon by Muslim communities. Once the necessary material was found, all materials were then surveyed for information that included the necessary perimeters of either a crucifixion, the crucifixion of Jesus, and or any suggested medical conditions associated with a crucifixion.

DATA EVALUATION

The search perimeters were set to only identify a Roman crucifixion; much of the data was included in this study. However, some of the material was not utilized because of overlapping information. For instance, if two authors described the same hypotheses, the third was not added. Moreover, contrasting hypotheses offered greater insight into refining the question that this study was designed for.

One hypostudy offered by Zugibe presented all of the possible circumstances for death in a typical crucifixion while landing on the theory that Jesus died from a ruptured heart. Although it was generally accepted as the leading cause of death, there were others who would argue for death by asphyxiation. Zugibe believed that the timing of Jesus's death and all that he went through would be more than likely a ruptured heart.[1]

What is medically accepted as possibilities for death in a crucifixion, the data included patients who expired from asphyxia, blunt force trauma, ruptured heart, and blood loss not during a crucifixion. Furthermore, if the data also included being revived from said conditions then the conditions produce a negative response. For example, if patient (a) died from blood loss, but was later revived by medical procedures or introduced to anything of the sort, that would mean that the individual was not accurately evaluated as deceased.

None of the data included in this study produced such results. There were patients who willfully agreed to undergo a crucifixion, while omitting the flogging aspect and being physically nailed to the wood. From these subjects, it was found that not many had difficulty breathing, and other medical complications, leading to the conclusion of crucifixion victims expiring from shock.

Such brutal methods from the Roman crucifixion could not be replicated by normal means of testing; therefore, the data from the Bible, mock crucifixion and archaeological findings produced the evidence to assert certain theories concerning the crucifixion of Jesus.

Analysis and Interpretation

Due to the lack of actually known crucifixion victims who were living during the time of the actual crucifixion, much of the

---

1. Zugibe, *Crucifixion of Jesus*, 120–21.

prescribed research was a view of all collective sources on the crucifixion of Jesus and others. Although Zugibe was able to recreate a crucifixion, it was not at the same description as what historical pieces of evidence state about the crucifixion. It would be morally challenged to have volunteers commit to such, to rest conclusion on mock testing is not a complete assessment.

The scope of this study is based purely on what is more plausible and more likely. Therefore, the data must reflect whether or not it was possible for Jesus to survive being crucified. What was interpreted thereafter was that the data collect proved it was not likely due to majority of research collectively gravitated to a cause of death, and not a cause of survival. Although the majority of research could not single out one condition as the prime reason for death, and neither research could not agree on said cause, the ultimate consensus was certain death.

PUBLIC PRESENTATION

Multiple letters were surveyed to signify the medical conclusions of the crucifixion. These are outlined in Fig. 1, the crux of which was provided by the Baylor University Medical Center's article, "Medical Views on the Death of Jesus Christ."[2]

Views on the Manner of Christ's Death	
Scholarly View	**Citations: First Author and Year (Chronological)**
Asphyxiation	LeBec, 1925; Whitaker, 1935; Mödder, 1948; Hynek, 1951; Furlong, 1952; Barbet, 1963; De-Pasquale, 1963; Bucklin, 1970; Lumpkin, 1978; Wassener, 1979; Jewell, 1979; Zias, 1985; Potter, 1986; Edwards, 1986; Blum, 1986; Thurston, 1987; Leinster, 1991; Bernardo, 1991; Porter, 1991; Holoubek, 1995; Metherell, 1998; Retief, 2003; Papaloucas, 2004; Eduard, 2017
Chiefly Asphyxiation With Secondary Factors	Sava, 1958; Davis, 1965; Miller, 2013; Bordes, 2020

2. Habermas et al., *Medical Views*, 751.

Views on the Manner of Christ's Death	
Scholarly View	**Citations: First Author and Year (Chronological)**
Cardiovascular Trauma	Stroud, 1847; Bersgma, 1948; Ball, 1989; Wright, 1991
Shock	Tenney, 1964; Zugibe, 2005; Bergeron, 2012, 2018
Coagulopathy	Brenner, 2005
Suspension Trauma	Schulte, 1963; Bishop, 2006
Syncope	Warren, 1986
No death	Davies, 1991; Ytrehus, 2002; Ledochowski, 2012, 2014

Through the information on this chart, it was determined that there was enough data to support the question of whether or not Jesus survived the cross. There were three individuals who argued against survival, and their response was appropriately noted.

CONCLUSION OF METHODS

The procedure utilized to collect all of the data from all noted parties was vetted by relevancy; data collected had to be within the nineteenth century and had to eliminate the possibility of biases. The data was then condensed to reduce redundancy, leaving only two or three scholars who would agree on the same topic. The following step would be to compile the remaining data and branch outwards from what those main sources stated, ensuring that the question that this study sought to ask was answered and the accusation was given a response.

The final step after the compilation of data was complete was to follow up with a rational answer to the hypostudy that reflected the known outcome. The known outcome would be either consistent with what Scripture states or what the Quran states.

3

Survey of Literature

SEVERAL COMPONENTS WILL BE discussed in this section regarding the story of Jesus—specifically concerning the crucifixion and resurrection. This chapter aims to get a general overview of what other scholars have ascertained, analyzed, and asserted concerning the crucifixion and resurrection of Jesus. Due to the nature of this chapter, whether or not God worked a miracle will not be argued; instead, it will offer the appraisals from scholars in different theological "parties" concerning Jesus, His crucifixion, and His resurrection. After reading this chapter, readers should have a general idea about where all the parties stand on the question of Jesus's crucifixion and resurrection, based on Scripture, logic, and physical evidence(s).

MUSLIM BELIEFS

One of the more dramatic explanations of Jesus's crucifixion and resurrection comes from Ahmed Deedat in his 1993 book, *Crucifixion or Cruci-fiction?* Originally just a pamphlet, Deedat's book does not follow what the Quran typically states about Jesus; rather, it utilizes the Christian Bible to justify its unorthodox claims and purposes.

Self-admittedly, the overall goal of Deedat's book is to educate the layman on how Jesus lived after being nailed to the cross. Also, it is essential to note that this particular literary work is an extension of what is commonly referred to as the Swoon Theory. Swoon Theory (or Apparent Death Theory) contains a number of ideas that point to the reason why Jesus might have survived the cross and that Jesus was merely unconscious when he was taken down from the cross.

After Jesus's "swooning," he remained in his tomb and later became conscious and left his tomb. The Apparent Death Theory eliminates the possibility of a miracle, the deity of Jesus Christ, and the Christian belief of a Savior who lives forever more. Although other apologists and evangelicals challenged the contents of Deedat's book (like Sam Shamoun[1] and Josh Mcdowell[2] in a recorded debate), the ideas throughout this book are still referred to by many people who favor this theory over what other literary works introduce.

The Ahmadiyya group preaches that Jesus never died on the cross; rather, he escaped to India to preach to the lost tribes of Israel. They recognize Jesus as a prophet of Allah and believe that Jesus could not meet the cross because his prime mission was to be the Messiah of Israel. Since the tribes of Israel were scattered, and Jesus's ministry was only in Judea, he could not complete his mission by staying and dying in Judea.[3] The way this group mimics the logic of Deedat and the Swoon Theory is in the idea that Jesus did not die on the cross, and the difference is only in approach. The majority of Deedat's approach to the crucifixion stems from how he interprets the Bible, but the Ahmadiyya Muslims utilize other kinds of literature developed by their members and supporters.[4]

According to Deedat, the spear to the side of Jesus actually rescued him. He said that Jesus was heavily fatigued and because people were held on the cross, this wound slowed down the blood

---

1. Shamoun, "Crucifixion of Christ," 62–63.
2. McDowell and Gilchrist, *Islam Debate*, 157–71.
3. Burhani, "Ahmadiyya and the Study," 148.
4. Joseph, "Jesus in India," 163.

circulation. So, because the spear was thrust into Jesus's side, it caused bloodletting, thus restoring circulation back to the heart and regaining rhythm.[5] Although this sounds medieval in its medical conclusion; however, this is what he and some others believe in their assertion of the crucifixion.

Scholars like Deedat, who have produced a similar version of the crucifixion, and have a strong following in the Muslim community. For instance, Shabir Ally, a Muslim apologist from the University of Toronto specializing in Quranic Exegesis, believes that the crucifixion has two meanings. He writes, "One meant to hang on a cross, but I believe that the word crucifixion is what the Quran means, which is to kill a person by that means."[6] Ally thinks that when the talked about the crucifixion, it meant that the punishment was not as severe as it was told. By no means is he stating that the Gospel accounts of Jesus's death are not significant. Rather, he (and others who agree with his assertion) acknowledge Jesus as a prophet of God who loved God.

In his book, *Demystifying Islam*, spokesman Zafar Harris addresses the issues surrounding Jesus. He states, "The verse from the Quran stating the mission of Jesus also contains an important passage, which clarifies the scope of his mission even further. It states that God sent Jesus 'as a Messenger to the Children of Israel,' which is a critical elucidation of why Jesus was sent by God to earth."[7]

On the matter of the crucifixion, Harris believes that Jesus was saved from death because, according to the Hebrew text, if anyone dies on the cross, he (or she) is accursed.[8] He furthers his idea by producing other theories that coincide together with Swoon Theorist Ally and the Ahmadiyya. Such views align with the substitution idea, which suggests that one of Jesus's disciples took the mantle of sacrificing himself in place of Jesus, which is warmly embraced in some circles.

5. Deedat, *Crucifixion or Cruci-Fiction*, 46.
6. Brierley, "Islam's Apologist."
7. Zafar, *Demystifying Islam*, 147.
8. Zafar, *Demystifying Islam*, 153.

According to Khaled M. Abou El Fadl,

> When Allah wanted to raise Jesus to heaven, Jesus went out to meet his followers at a house where all his twelve disciples assembled. He went out to them from a well in the house, and his hair was dripping with water. He said, "Among you are those who will disbelieve in me twelve times even after having believed in me." Then he added, "Which one of you agrees to look like me and be killed in my place and enjoy the status reserved for me with my Lord?" Their youngest stood up, but Jesus told him to sit down. He repeated the question to them, and the same young man stood up again, whereupon Jesus said, "Then you shall be the one." He was immediately made to look just like Jesus, then Jesus was raised to heaven. The Jews came and took the disciple who looked just like Jesus, killed him, then crucified him.[9]

Clearly, the Muslim camp acknowledges that Jesus existed and that he was religious figure, but unfortunately, that is as far as it goes. Any attempt to share the Christian message that Jesus died on the cross and was resurrected by God on the third day is met with various objections or theories promoting a heterodox story. In many ways, the Muslim assertions appear to align themselves with gnostic gospels suggesting heterodox stories of Jesus's ministry and death.

Swoon Theory

In order to understand Swoon Theory (also known as the Apparent Death Theory), it would be prudent to look at some of the reasons why it was created. One of the prime reasons that the Swoon Theory originated was in response to the Christian doctrine regarding the resurrection of Jesus Christ. The Christian belief affirms that Jesus Christ was more than just a prophet of Yahweh; instead, He is the risen Son of God, and by him, those who believe in him will

9. Fadl, *Great Theft*, 82.

be saved and gifted with eternal life under Christ (according to John 3:16).

The Swoon Theory sought to correct the idea that God had resurrected Jesus. The Quran affirms explicitly that Jesus did not die on the cross; however, this theory is not a settled matter for other scholars. There is historical evidence that contributes to the idea that Jesus was crucified. It would appear that the Swoon theory further promotes and rationalizes what the Quran states. It is battling its way through the western ideology and trying to do what the Quran does not provide—proof that Jesus did not die on the cross.

Furthermore, the Swoon Theory engages with what Paul stated in 1 Corinthians 15:14—if Christ has not been raised from the dead, any preaching, faith, and Christianity as a worldview are all in vain. The people of the Muslim faith find some solidarity in the Swoon Theory because it argues that Jesus Christ was never raised from the dead. Instead, the orthodox Gospel message, this theory attempts to suggest the possibility that Jesus was either swapped out with one of his disciples, that Jesus "played possum," that Jesus was on the brink of death and was resuscitated because of the spear, or was in a coma-like state when he was placed in the tomb.

Essentially, if it was proven that Jesus Christ never raised from the dead, then more arguments could be made that Jesus Christ was not the Son of God. This would align more with traditional Islamic thought. According to the Quranic boast in Sura 4:157–158:

> We have killed the Christ Jesus, son of Mary, God's messenger. They did not kill him, and neither did they crucify him, but it only seemed to them as if it had been so. Those who hold conflicting views about him are indeed confused, having no real knowledge about it and following mere conjecture. For, of a certainty, they did not kill him.[10]

---

10. Salahi, *The Qur'an*, 62.

The irony is that Salahi is suggesting that he knows more in certainty about what happened some six hundred years after it happened than those who were actually present at the time of the events or even at the moment and time of Jesus's death, such as the Apostles or historians like Tacitus.

Although the Swoon Theory offers a great point that no physician verified if Jesus was, in fact, dead (an argument from silence), there are still some significant issues surrounding this hypostudy. Professor of Arabic and Religion Sherene Khouri writes that the Swoon Theory was fashioned a long time ago, but contrary to the arguments by Christian apologists, it still holds merit.[11] Canadian Islamic preacher Shabir Ally also believes that there are multiple meanings for the word, *crux*.

The *crux* or *staurōs* appears approximately thirty-three times in Scripture, all referring to the means of capital punishment and execution. Oher researchers of biblical literature have accepted that the *crux* was not something to be taken lightly or meaning something other than death. Although Ally's theory attempts to present a solution to prove that Jesus did not die on the cross, the ultimate goal is believed to find reasons not to believe in the risen Christ because if Christ rose, it would destroy the Muslim faith.

According to Habermas, the Swoon Theory tries to assert itself as a historical fact; however, the historical facts all point to the reality that a prophet and healer named Jesus did die on a cross in the first century and was said to have risen from the dead by his followers (and even those outside of Judaism and Christianity).[12] Therefore, if the Swoon Theory is false, it will further the claim that Jesus is God's Son, and their faith affirmation is lacking without Christ.

Scholars like Ahmed Deedat have brought some intriguing ideas concerning the Swoon Theory in his book, but since he supports what the Quran says, it is necessary to examine what the Quran itself says about the matter (see chapter four for more

---

11. Khouri, "Crucifixion in the Qur'an," 162.
12. Habermas, *Risen Jesus*, 9.

information). For now, this study will focus on what the Jewish scholars contributed to this area of interest.

THE JEWISH PERSPECTIVE

Jesus Christ is not only a topic for Christians and Muslims but is also for the Jewish people. Whenever people hear of works from those of the Jewish faith, their topics revolve around the *Torah* or the *Tanakh*. The *Torah* is the first body of works of Moses, Genesis, Exodus, Leviticus, Numbers, and Deuteronomy. The *Tanakh* is the body of works containing all the Old Testament, including the twelve minor prophets, and connecting books like 1 and 2 Chronicles as one book. There was another body of works written after the death of Jesus called the *Talmud*. The Talmud talks about Jesus and the Jews' issues with his teachings and power. Solomon Zeitlin discovered that there were different circles within the Jewish circle during the time of Jesus. These separate groups were the Sadducees, Pharisees, and the Essenes.

The Sadducees (academics and theologians) were some of the High Priests who held office after the death of Herod. The Pharisees (cultural and political rabbis) were given the name Pharisees (Perushim) as a term of reproach. The reason behind this was that the Sadducees believed in the written law of the Torah, which did not include any talk of resurrection. However, the Pharisees did believe in the resurrection, and this idea spread among the people, like Martha in John 11:24. The resurrection appeared to be common knowledge among the people.

The Essenes, according to historian Joan Taylor, were not mentioned in the Gospels specifically but noted that they were autonomous and allowed to live their lives subject to their own interpretation of Mosaic law.[13] The Essenes appear to be very important, and with the writings of Josephus and the Dead Sea Scrolls, scholars now have a better idea of who the Essenes were. The Essenes were reported to be either driven out or left of their

13. Taylor, *Essenes*, 109.

own volition to the caves and established Qumran as their desert retreat settlement, only to be threatened by the Romans during a Jewish revolt against Rome in 66–73 CE. This is also where the Essenes deposited their library until it was found centuries later.[14] If what Crawford says is true about the Essenes, then they would be present during the time of the crucifixion; however, whether the Essenes believed about the resurrection (like other teachers of the law) is outside the scope of this investigation.

American Jewish historian Solomon Zeitlin also stated that the Talmud, Josephus, and the book of Acts all substantiated the idea that the Pharisees believed in resurrection, providence, reward, and punishment, but the Sadducees denied all of these things.[15] Solomon wondered if the Sanhedrin convicted Jesus, why did they have to bring him before Pilate and accuse him? They had the right to carry out the death sentence. His theory is that Jesus was a problem for the Jews and their relationship with the Romans, which is why they had to bring him to Pilate. This seems plausible since the Sanhedrin was able to pronounce judgments on their own people.

The Apostle Paul was able to evade Jewish judgment by calling attention to his Roman citizenship, while Jesus, on the other hand, was afforded such an opportunity. However, if Jesus was truly a problem for the Romans, the Sanhedrin offered the Romans the opportunity to deal with one who transgressed against Caesar. Jesus, who is the King, would rival Caesar and any other power going forward (Rom 14:11, Isa 45:23, and Rev 1:5). The Sanhedrin did not desire to cause problems with the superpower nation at that time, regardless of how much the Jews preferred to be liberated from their rule, without the Messiah, liberation from the tyranny of the Romans was impossible (Acts 1:6).

The religious issues of Jesus did not concern the Sanhedrin— only that he was a political offender, which is why Roman soldiers came to arrest Jesus.[16] Solomon's theory is trying to vindicate the

14. Crawford, *Scribes and Scrolls*, 4.

15. Zeitlin, "Crucifixion of Jesus," 330.

16. Zeitlin, "Crucifixion of Jesus," 362.

Jews of the responsibility of killing Jesus, which the Jews were accused of for many years. The Talmud, Josephus, and the Gospels (Matt 25:27) all tell that Jesus was crucified, which is not rejected by all Jewish scholars, and the Quran states that the Jews believed that they were responsible for killing Jesus.

Peter Schäfer created an exhaustive study called *Jesus in the Talmud*. Schäfer states, "The figure of Jesus does appear in the Talmud, as does his mother Mary—not in a coherent narrative, but scattered throughout the rabbinic literature, in general, and the Talmud in particular and often dealt with in passing, in conjunction with another subject pursued as the major theme."[17] Schäfer also believes that the stories about Jesus and his family in the Babylonian texts only serve as a counter-narrative to what the Gospels state.

Looking through the Talmud, readers will find much of Babylonian culture within it and how they dealt with the law of Yahweh. The Jewish leaders would have *clauses* that would help them get around the law of Moses, which the Gospels highlight whenever Jesus would rebuke the teachers of the law. A perfect example of this happening is reflected in Matthew 23, when Jesus addresses the hypocrisy of the Pharisees.

According to Shäfer, the Pharisees subverted the Christian idea of Jesus's resurrection by having him punished forever in hell and by making clear that this fate awaits his followers as well, who believe in this impostor.[18] The imposter was one of the names referring to Jesus, and one can also ascribe the name, Balaam (Βαλαάμ), which means "false teacher" and "not of the people." Therefore, when one reads in the Sanhedrin 106b,

> A certain heretic said to Rabbi Hanina: Have you heard how old Balaam was when he died? Rabbi Hanina said to him: It is not written explicitly in the Torah. But from the fact that it is written: "Bloody and deceitful men shall not live half their days" (Psalms 55:24), this indicates that he was thirty-two or thirty-four years old, less than half

17. Schäfer, *Jesus in the Talmud*, 15.
18. Schäfer, *Jesus in the Talmud*, 23.

the standard seventy-year lifespan. The heretic said to him: You have spoken well, I myself saw the notebook of Balaam, and it was written therein: Balaam the lame was thirty-two years old when Pinehas the highwayman killed him.[19]

Ergo, it is commonplace that many modern Jews reject Jesus of Nazareth as the Messiah.

Johnathan Bernis stated that the modern concept of the Messiah in Judaism is a complex issue, but what is clear and undisputed among most Jews is that Jesus was not the Messiah.[20] In the Old Testament, there are several Scriptures that talk about the Messiah that should be mentioned. Passages like Numbers 24:17–19, Psalm 60:7, and Isaiah 42:1–4 all talk about the Messiah being the scepter of Judah and the savior of Israel who will bring justice. Since Jesus did not unshackle the Jews from the Roman empire, the leaders did not believe that he was the Messiah. This could be the reason why, in the New Testament, the leaders wanted to see more signs and wonders, and ironically the question about whether Jesus came from Judah does not appear to be the problem due to the census mentioned in Luke 2.

This Jewish audience appears to accept responsibility for protecting their way of life against what the Christian movement believes. While Bernis is a Jewish Christian, he only states what (and how) he was taught as a child. On a different but similar side of the Jewish spectrum, there are the Messianic Jews.

Messianic Jews are ethnically Jewish; however, what separates them from the others in Judaism is that they believe that Jesus of Nazareth is the Messiah promised to the Jewish people. Following centuries of persecution and anti-Semitism by Christians, most Jewish people no longer accept Messianic Jews as Jewish, believing that they have become gentiles.[21]

Hillel Newman finds some similarities between the Gospel accounts and the *Toledot Yeshu* regarding Jesus's trial and crucifixion

19. Eisenstein, "Sanhedrin 106B:2."
20. Jonathan, *Rabbi Looks*, 141.
21. Morgan, *Understanding World Religions*, 61.

that is worthy of submission. He recounts the stories of Jesus dying in a cabbage patch by means of the crucifixion, according to the *Toledot* literature. Before his death, Jesus's dealings with Pilate are also briefly mentioned. Moreover, Newman also discovers information about Pilate's sentencing and execution of Jesus. He states, "In *Ada Pilati IX*, 5 (425 CE), Pilate passes sentence and decrees to Jesus 'that you should first be scourged according to the law of the pious emperors, and then hanged on the cross in the garden where you were seized.'"[22]

Generally, Jewish executions did not include crucifixions. They typically employed stoning or burning instead, according to the Mishnah.[23] Hillel believes that these stories depict what the gnostic Jews believe happened with Jesus, which falls in line with the fact that Jesus died, instead of what the Swoon Theorists (and the other Muslim supporters of the Ahmadiyya) believe happened.

Historically, scholars can only affirm that Jesus died on the cross but somehow was seen later because historical evidence from all testimonies cannot absolutely confirm Jesus's miracle claims. Although the fact that Jesus died and that he was seen later points to a miracle in the Christian worldview, the Judaic worldview limits their understanding that Jesus is the living King forevermore.

A worldview can limit a person's understanding of a subject. For instance, a Christian with a biblical worldview would think differently about recent LGBT marriage laws passed in America, but a person with an atheist worldview might not perceive the issues that come with such laws on a spiritual and physical level. Therefore, with this topic of Jesus dying on the cross at the hands of the Romans and Jews who said, "Crucify him!" many Christians would acknowledge that God raised Jesus Christ from the dead, and that he is sitting on the right hand of the Father. Furthermore, a Christian theist would further support the historical claims to evangelical/biblical truths.

22. Morgan, *Understanding World Religions*, 61.
23. Goldin, *Hebrew Criminal Law*, 28–36.

CHRISTIAN THEISM

As this study shifts away from the Jewish circle (which proved advantageous to the study of Jesus, the crucifixion, and his deity), a natural trajectory would be toward the Christian camp. When looking at the Christian camp, one cannot talk about the historical Jesus without mentioning Apologist Gary Habermas. Habermas looks at the crucifixion story from a historical perspective, which is significant given the limitation of the time gap. Habermas affirms that the crucifixion was a common form of execution employed by the Romans for various classes of people, including treason.[24]

When it comes to the case of Jesus (and his crucifixion), the Gospels and other non-biblical sources (like Josephus or Tacitus) reinforce the assertion that Jesus was executed on the cross.[25] Habermas states that the reality of Jesus dying on the cross was the quintessential aspect in his case for the resurrection miracle. Despite historical testimonies, it is clear that many Muslims doubt that Jesus was crucified.

When looking at the facts surrounding the crucifixion of Jesus, Darrell Bock asserts that the Romans were the only ones legally able to execute within the lands—not the Jews. The most severe rite of execution, crucifixion, was a power Rome that kept solely for itself. Crucifixion was not only an aspect of the rule of law against criminals but also an expression of political power and a reminder of that power by example.[26]

Generally, what one finds in Christian scholarship (in the case of Jesus) is more of a historical study. This could be because of the allocations raised concerning the resurrection miracle. Regardless of the reason, one can historically believe that Jesus existed and was crucified under Roman law. One of the allegations that Christian theists face (then and now) is that the Jesus story was a later invention by Paul or the disciples.

---

24. Habermas and Licona, *Case for the Resurrection*, 48.
25. Josephus, "Antiquities 18.64."
26. Bock, *Studying the Historical*, 120.

One of the most significant issues with this theory is that Paul (Saul of Tarsus) was a persecutor of the early believers of Jesus. So, why would Paul invent a story about Jesus that would further the doctrine of Jesus? This is an essential question because much of the New Testament is filled with writings from this former prosecutor. It was this former chief of sinners, according to 1 Timothy 1:15, who believed that Jesus Christ died and was resurrected so much that he was willing to die sharing those beliefs. Darrell Bock traces the date of death for Jesus through Paul's conversion. This means that Paul's conversion is key to narrowing down when the crucifixion and resurrection happened.

William Lane Craig recounts a typical crucifixion as being humiliating, painful, and for Jewish prophets, a curse. He writes, "A Messiah who failed to deliver and to reign, who was defeated, humiliated, and slain by His enemies, is a contradiction in terms. Nowhere do Jewish texts speak of such a 'Messiah.'"[27] Craig also notes that after Jesus's crucifixion, all the disciples could do was wait with longing for the general resurrection of the dead to see their Master again.[28] Craig retells a hopeless story to render all doubt that Jesus could have survived the cross. This same line of thinking is present in most Christian circles.

The process of the crucifixion was a gruesome, painful, embarrassing event. Craig also finds some validity in McCane's study on Jesus's burial. The burial is significant because: 1. It shows from history that Jesus did die. 2. It shows that the type of crucifixion was more than just humiliation in view of Jesus's peers. 3. It shows that there is historical data that leads to the conclusion that Jesus went through a painful crucifixion, and his burial was known by Jewish leaders as others during that time.[29]

Christian theists recognize the need for Jesus Christ to have been sacrificed on the cross. Genesis 3 marks the time when humanity became in debt to God. Adam and Eve decided to disobey God's command and ate from the tree of knowledge of good and

27. Craig, *On Guard*, 241.

28. Craig, *On Guard*, 241.

29. Craig, "Jesus Buried," 404–9.

evil. Adam and Eve had pride, they desired exaltation, but it was undue exaltation, and they lost the connection they once had with God and each other.[30] Their actions caused humanity to be consumed with wages of sin.

Looking at the crucifixion event itself, one could wonder why the Roman government would be so interested in a Jew who was going around teaching and healing. As mentioned earlier, the Sanhedrin had the full authority to execute transgressors of Jewish law, so why place the focus on Rome? Christian theist Mark Smith suggests thar Pilate knew little about Jesus, indicating that Jesus possibly was not a problem for Rome; rather, he was an issue for the Jewish leadership and how they dealt with their people.[31] Jesus corrected the teachings of the Jewish leaders, drove the merchants out of the temple, and pointed out that the teachers of the law were stumbling blocks to the kingdom of God. Moreover, the Roman empire did not know (or care) about the prophecy of a Messiah, the coming of the Son of man, and of a king who would reign, eternally. Still, the fact that Jesus was crucified by the Romans suggests that the impact of the Son of Man would be more for the world than just for the Jews, locally.

NATURALISM BELIEFS

From a historical perspective, the naturalist might have different rules that they would utilize than other historians, but on the subject of miracles, this would not be a plausible or sensible conclusion on their end. Why so many historians could arrive at different conclusions is due to what they view as their horizon. By horizon, it meant their convictions, beliefs, biases, and worldviews. For instance, David Hume wrote about what would qualify as evidence for what transpired in the past; however, those same qualifications are rooted in the naturalistic circle. Inside this same circle is what

---

30. Boice, *Foundations*, 197.
31. Smith, *Final Days of Jesus*, 181.

is allowed to exist, and what exists is more than likely explainable by what is generally known and seen.

Hume delighted in his argument against miracles, stating, "I flatter myself, that I have discovered an argument of a like nature, which, if just, will, with the wise and learned, be an everlasting check to all kinds of superstitious delusion, and consequently, will be useful as long as the world endures."[32] Hume said no testimony is sufficient to establish a miracle unless the testimony is of such a kind that its falsehood would be more miraculous than the fact, which it endeavors to establish; and even in that case, there is a mutual destruction of arguments, and the superior only gives us an assurance suitable to that degree of force, which remains, after deducting the inferior[33]

For the naturalist who is operating under Hume's line of thinking, testimonies from witnesses are of no value, and if the situation has not happened in his lifetime, it is not possible that it ever occurred in the past. Now, the reason why miracles are mentioned at this stage is only to highlight the conclusion that historically Jesus died and was seen later, which would lead to something miraculous.

The crucifixion, more specifically, is taken through eyewitness testimonies, and even under Hume's qualifications, there appears to be no scholar who accepts that Jesus did die on the cross. Why is this allowed in the naturalist community? The reason is simply that, at this point, this study is only discussing what happened historically and not about miracles. Also, there are accounts from the enemies of Jesus that agree that Jesus was executed on the cross and died by means of crucifixion did happen, which flows with Hume's criteria.

---

32. Hume, "Of Miracles," 30.

33. Licona, *Resurrection of Jesus*, 136.

The Medical Perspective

As previously indicated, the majority of parties in this chapter believe that Jesus died on the cross. Swoon Theory, or the Apparent Death Theory, has argued that Jesus survived the cross; therefore, it would be prudent to observe how one dies on the cross from a medical perspective. The medical camp originates from a place of science, where hypotheses must come from reason or the scientific method. The scientific method is where the researcher would ask a question or observation, hypothesize about the answer, make a prediction about the outcome, and from their studies and profession in their respective fields; they would then draw conclusions from whatever mach-tests were created. Therefore, it would be safe to trust their medical advice covering this matter.

Scholars like Frederick Zugibe contributed to a study on the ruptured heart theory. In his 2005 book, *The Crucifixion of Jesus A Forensic Inquiry*, Zugibe said that the Ruptured Heart Theory is unlikely due to the age of Jesus and the time it would take to cause blood and water to flow out. The Ruptured Heart Theory was advanced by William Stroud in 1874 when he suggested that Jesus's heart ruptured, and the blood flowed into the sac surrounding the heart, called the pericardium, resulting in the blood and water flowing out of Jesus.[34] He also believes that one rare complication of a heart attack is the rupture of the heart. It usually occurs in individuals who suffered either a silent heart attack, chest pains they believed were due to indigestion or some other cause, or direct trauma to the heart.[35]

Zugibe thinks that the cause of death is more likely to be a hypovolemic shock. Other examiners have their opinions as to the cause of death by crucifixion dating back to almost the 1800s. Stroud believed death by crucifixion was due to cardiac rupture in 1847, but Zugibe refuted that cause and believed that it was a hypovolemic shock in 2005, while again in 2005, a hematologist

---

34. Stroud, *Treatise on the Physical*, 85.
35. Zugibe, *Crucifixion of Jesus*, 125.

named Edwards thought it was a pulmonary embolism.[36] The key is all of these medical experts have contributed to how one would die from a Roman crucifixion, and all of them in their respective professions never agreed that someone would medically survive the cross without extensive medical attention.

From the medical perspective, most theories come from what some Roman antiquities report about a crucifixion, the Gospels (which have more detail about the crucifixion), and other medical journals that are closely related to hanging, flogging, and impaling. Although it is limited in how far forensics can reach back in time, it has the same outcome as historians. One must rely on written testimonies, experiences from others, archaeological finds, and what is known medically then and today. Regardless of the limitations, the outcome remains that the position of medical advisers, no matter the originating theory, arrives at the same conclusion—that Jesus died on the cross and had no chance to survive this ordeal.

CONSIDERATIONS

After surveying literature from the aforementioned respective groups, it is clear that a significant number of theories exist surrounding Jesus and his crucifixion. However, the Muslim camp appears to be the main one asserting that Jesus did not die on the cross, despite the historical evidence and testimonies. Leaning on an oversimplified premise, the Muslim circle supposes that Jesus was not crucified because in the law of Moses (Deut 21:22–23) God only allows an individual to be hung on the cross if they were cursed. As Jesus was known to be a prophet of Allah, he could not possibly be cursed and forsaken by Allah. Unfortunately, their theory does not follow historically what other circles have found, despite those circles having nothing to gain, ostensibly, by affirming the crucifixion.

The Jewish circle provided challenging comments on the crucifixion. They believe that Jesus did die on the cross, but they are

---

36. Maslen and Mitchell, "Medical Theories," 186.

under the impression that it was well deserved. If Jesus was a false prophet who claimed that he was equal to God, then, by all means, the Jews could be right in their judgment call. However, if the Jews were wrong and that they rejected the Son of God, the promised Messiah, the true King, then the result would be disastrous. For the Jews, the Messiah was supposed to rid their enemies, which at that time would have been Rome. Jesus, on the other hand, was meek, humble, righteous, and just.

Jesus's concerns, per the Gospels, were not concerned with overthrowing the people of Rome; rather, he was interested in changing the hearts of the children of Israel. The children of Israel were told to repent (Matt 4:17), to change their thinking and prepare for a culture change in the kingdom of heaven. The way Jesus came, the manner in which he taught, and the type of people to whom he ministered caused some of the Jewish people to reject him. It could be stated that some of the Jews are still awaiting the Messiah, but the main point is that many Jewish circles believe that Jesus died on the cross and was cursed by God.

The Christian circle presented an argument from history to prove that Jesus is the promised Messiah who was sacrificed on the cross. Their argument was to investigate the miracle claim through historical evidence, though historical evidence has some limitations. However, such limitations as time are helped by the sources at their disposal. Specific sources like texts, writings, perspectives from friends and enemies, eyewitness testimonies, and archaeological finds made it possible to further the discussion on whether Jesus died and whether he was seen later.

One example of this is the Shroud of Turin, which is an archaeological discovery that helps people see evidence of the crucifixion. However, the shroud has been under scientific scrutiny because it was believed that it was a forgery from the medieval period. Some blood specialists have found traces of DNA that resemble some of the properties of blood, like iron and zinc, but no overwhelming conclusions were formulated for the resounding yes. In 2017, Liberato De Caro and Cinzia Giannini reported that through digital restoration, the shroud does not point to a medieval invention but to a man who was crucified alive.[37] Furthermore, since digital imaging is acceptable for retracing historical events, this method should be taken seriously and help guide individuals to a clear answer for the authenticity of the shroud.

Another historical discovery is found, and not found, when discussing that there is an empty tomb. There are locations that were excavated, according to the rules of the presiding government, for the possible location for the burial of Jesus Christ. All of the possible locations were empty, which led to two possibilities. One is that the archaeologists were in the wrong location. However, it is unlikely that multiple archaeologists were in the wrong location because information concerning the burial of Jesus is known by Jews and could be tracked by reviewing several collaborating historical documents. This leaves inquirers with the results of number two, which is that the tomb was empty because Jesus had risen from the dead.[38]

The evidence presented from history appears to support the narrative of the Gospels. The question that follows is if the inquirers trust the evidence presented as the Christians do and as the early church did. If the answer is a resounding yes, regarding if Jesus was dead, then seen again, the likelihood of a miraculous event taking place is in favor of what Christian theists believe. As with the naturalist, they will hold to the belief that miracles are not possible, but what is possible is that someone will die if flogged and then executed by crucifixion.

Their only reservations would purely be in the resurrection as a form of divine action. However, at this stage of the conversation, all this study is discussing is the likelihood of Jesus surviving the cross and being seen as healthy and walking around with his disciples later. Therefore, the answer is naturally impossible unless the historical Jesus was switched before the ordeal. However, historically this did not happen.

So, when one focuses on the question of how one can expire by crucifixion, the medical camp presents key solutions. Due to

---

37. De Caro and Giannini, "Turin Shroud Hands," 144.

38. Smith, *Was the Tomb Empty*, 57–60.

the multitude of ideas presented by medical experts, this study concludes that could be a multi-causality of medical justifications for dying on the cross, but none points to survival. Since none of the possibilities point towards survival, even with the herbs and spices brought during the burial of Jesus, he still would have needed to undergo several surgical operations that were not developed until centuries afterward; thus leaving Jesus dead until God rose him from the dead.

4

Apologetical Appraisal

CHRISTIAN APOLOGETICS DEALS WITH the defense or answer to a question or understanding concerning Christianity, its beliefs, and its relationship to the Bible. The resurrection of Jesus Christ is one of the most remarkable events to ever happen in history, as such, some hold to the impossibility of this miraculous event. Therefore, by discussing the crucifixion, it is the hope of believers of Christ to bring some clarity and understanding (and finally acceptance of Jesus Christ as Lord and Savior), ultimately placing into practice the qualities and values of a follower of Christ (2 Pet 1:10–11).

This chapter will cover several categories regarding apologetics. Although the previous chapter gave some context on some of the roles of these different approaches, this chapter dives deeper into how a classical apologist, an evidentialist, and presuppositional apologist would engage in this particular conversation on the crucifixion of Jesus. No approach is fully sufficient, but all offer outstanding perspectives with the hope of directing people toward the truth of the Gospel of Jesus Christ.

THE STARTING POINT

Considering the crucifixion, the first part of the discussion is to address who Jesus Christ actually is. Without this information or acceptance of the truth concerning Jesus Christ, then the conversation is laid on deaf ears. However, the answer to this question is rather complex for those who do not hold to the Christian faith; therefore, this section will only discuss what Scripture announces about Jesus as the Son of the Living God, and what Jesus also affirms in Scripture.

According to Hebrews 5:5, Jesus is named High Priest who was appointed by God. Jesus receives this title because He is the Son and because He is the only one qualified to be an advocate and mediator for humanity. Since Jesus is the High Priest forever, according to verse six, Jesus would have to be eternal.

Being eternal also gives the reader of Hebrews insight into the deity of Jesus. Allen remarks in his commentary that the author of Hebrews makes a clear distinction between the Levitical priesthood and Jesus, and then returns to Psalm 2:7 to signify the supremacy of Christ.[1] Since Jesus is the Son, there are some who believe that God had intercourse with Mary. However, when Scripture says the word, "begotten" (referring to Christ), the Gospel of John interjects that Christ was in the beginning during creation. Furthermore, all things were created through him because He is the Word, according to John 1:1–4.

Eternality and not being created are attributes only attributed to God. The angels were created, and humanity, the universe, and the laws of nature were created, but not Christ. Christ cannot be Alpha and Omega (noting supremacy) and be created. The argument that a classical apologist would strive to promote would be formed by noting of God's justice and righteousness, which led to the need of Christ. Sproul talked about this very subject in his book, *The Truth of the Cross*.[2]

---

1. Allen, *Hebrews*, 319.
2. Sproul, *Truth of the Cross*, 10.

The first truth is to accept that atonement is absolutely necessary. Why is atonement quintessential, and why should Christians and the world accept this as fact? The reason behind that is God is just and righteous.[3] God has never comprised justice or righteousness for anything or anyone. God is holy and omni-virtuous; therefore, the atonement was not something by chance or unnecessary, or hypothetically necessary. The fall of man, as told in the Genesis narrative, caused humanity to fall under the judgement and debt of sin—which is under the judgment of God by His righteousness.

Anselm published a work titled, *Cur Deus Homo*, in which he meant to provide a response to the question: Why is Jesus the God-man? Why is Christ necessary, and ultimately, why the cross? Anselm believed that the reason Christ in flesh was essential was because of the justice of God. He wrote, "As sin, the cause of our condemnation, had its origins from a woman, so ought the author of our righteousness and salvation to be born of a woman."[4]

Throughout his book, Anselm gives his response according to what is known about God, his righteousness, his perfection, his justice, and his holiness. He concludes, "He cannot excuse sin. Rather, He must pass judgment on it. The Judge of all the earth must do right. Therefore, He must punish the sinners—or provide a way to atone for their sin."[5]

When the world rejects that atonement is necessary, the cross becomes unnecessary. Orthodox Christianity resembles this knowledge within their doctrine, leading the classical apologist to lead with this as the foundation of their very argument. God is just, and sin must be judged. Sin cannot be overlooked by God and needs to be answered.

Therefore, the cross is crucial for salvation, but why the God-man? Could not a man like Abraham, Jacob, or Joseph, or even Job (who was called righteous) take the mantle of savior? Apparently not, for Romans 3:23 states that all peope have sinned, and all have failed the standards of God. This includes those mentioned in

3. Sproul, *Truth of the Cross*, 19.
4. Anselm and Deane, *Cur Deus Homo*, 21.
5. Sproul, *Truth of the Cross*, 28.

Scripture as the patriarchs of Old Testament, and even the disciples and apostles in the New Testament. So, God (being omniscient) knew that all of man was doomed. Just as Sodom and Gomorrah was judged and then destroyed, so would the rest of humanity if God did not provide an escape.

Jesus, as God-man, is vital for humanity because only someone who was not guilty, and without sin, could cover the debt of the world's sin. The model that was required for all humanity was told in Genesis to Adam. God said that on the day Adam and Eve disobeyed and ate from the tree of knowledge of good and evil, they would surely die. The next course of judgment was blood because Adam did indeed sin.

As time went on, the sins of humanity increased, thus creating the need of a savior to fulfill the debt requirement—once and for all. The key thing to note is that God provided the judgment and the solution to a man-unsolvable problem—hence, the need for the God-man to come and be sacrificed for the world.

Christology

In theology, the study of the person of Jesus Christ is called Christology. This deals with the person, His works, and who He is in all aspects. At the very heart of Christology is the crucifixion, for without the crucifixion and resurrection of Jesus Christ, this teaching would be meaningless. Classical apologists like R.C. Sproul, Anselm of Canterbury, and St. Augustine would more than likely engage the importance of the cross from different angles, but ultimately resolve on the point that the cross was necessary, and it defines the love, mercy, perfect will, judgement, and righteousness of God. However, without talking about the person of Christ, some will not grasp the intricate details of the cross.

This is where Christology comes into the picture. In Reformation Christology, Jean Calvin believed that the Bible was the authority on religious matters and believed that Christ is one person with two distinct natures:[6] one divine and one human. The same view of the reformers like Calvin on matters of atonement followed what Anselm believed about atonement, meaning that Christ died to satisfy the justice of God—rightfully, because no human alive or past could appease the justice of God.

A Classical Apologist would connect the justice of God, and then compare it to some judge who would rule with some integrity, fairness, and not known for corruptness. A judge would rule for punishment on those who are guilty. No matter the circumstances of the crime, the person remains guilty of sin in the eyes of God. For instance, if a man was brought before the court for stealing bread, and the man told the court that he stole the bread to feed his family. While some judges could overlook the crime, it is still a sin to steal.

Going back to Genesis, Adam tried to shift the blame, not just to avoid responsibility, but because he was still guilty. Therefore, judgment had to be satisfied, but because God is merciful, patient, and loving, God provided an out for humanity. So, the classical apologist, after proving the existence of God by means of one of the notable arguments like the Designer Argument,[7] would have to convince the audience that because God exists and He is a righteous judge, Christ being crucified is essential for humanity's welfare.

A PROVOCATIVE PERSPECTIVE

Since God is all-knowing, God knew that humanity would never be able to pay the debt of sin. God was very aware of the finite capabilities of man. Therefore, Jesus had to come as one who was the perfect sacrifice that would cover all of humanity's sin. Another

---

6. Enns, *Moody Handbook of Theology*, 481.

7. This argument suggests that the universe (and all life within it) were created with a purpose and function that notes that creation was not happenstance. Therefore, a cosmological designer must exist, transcendent of the universe, possessing the intelligence and power to realize cosmic fine-tuning and willfully act regarding the design. See Sober, *The Design Argument* (2018).

part of God's nature must deal with his mercy and lovingkindness. It was only through God's love and charity that He allowed His one and only Son to be crucified, to be slaughtered like a lamb, and to be hung on the cross. Jesus, in essence, was the embodiment of the love and mercy of God (Isa 53:10).

The nature of Christ is really no difference than the Father because He and the Father are one. Jesus is patient, loving, righteous, and holy. Without the cross, man cannot be justified. Theologian R.C. Sproul wrote, "The only works of righteousness that serve to justify a sinner are the works of Christ. So, when one says that people are justified by faith alone, it is meant that people are justified by Christ alone, by His works; human works do not count toward one's justification.[8]

As it stands, if Jesus did not die on the cross, then it would be no benefit for humanity to serve God, because no one can know the Father except through the Son. However, this section poses this argument: what would one lose if Jesus was not the answer? They would ultimately lose nothing, because Jesus commanded all to serve God with all one's heart, soul, and mind to "love one another as we love ourselves." However, the cost would be an agonizing death if Jesus was the answer, and one did not choose Christ.

The Muslim party recognizes Jesus as a prophet of God; all that Jesus was and did must be adhered to, because of his authority. So, it costs more to not follow Jesus who is, who was, and is to come, as promised in the book of Revelation, and throughout the New Testament. The question is whether a person is willing to risk the eternity of peace under the headship of Christ.

THE CLASSICAL APOLOGETICAL UNDERSTANDING

Apologetics has been utilized since the first-century church by the Apostles. Evidence of this could be found in Acts 17:22–32 and 1 Peter 3:15–16. Shortly after the apostles died, Christianity still had

---

8. Sproul, *Can I Be Sure*, 13–14.

to be prepared to provide a defense for what followers believed. However, not only did Christians have to defend their beliefs concerning the man, Jesus of Nazareth, but also his deity as the Triune God. Christians further found themselves having to defend the truth that God exists. Thus, classical apologetics is a method that begins by first utilizing various theistic arguments such as the cosmological or teleological arguments to establish the existence of God.[9] The cosmological argument is more about causality and the cause of existence, while the teleological argument is the evidence for an intelligent designer.

An example of the cosmological argument would be observing the universe. The universe had a cause, if it had a cause, there is naturally a beginning, which would point to God. For the teleological argument, it would be like the watch maker argument. An intelligent maker would had to create all that this world knows about nature, being God.

In Christianity, all things start and end with Christ because he is God—according to the accounts of the Gospels and other Old and New Testament scriptural proofs. For instance, it would be prudent for a classical apologist to start in Genesis, the creation narrative, to signify the importance of God, Christ, and the Holy Spirit. The classical apologist takes the Bible as the authority and utilizes other sources to strengthen their argument. Furthermore, he addresses the unbeliever with fundamental truths at the starting point.

Presuppositionalism

For the presuppositional apologist, the conversation takes a rather different route. It could be said that the classical apologist seeks to prove Christian theology from the outside in, while the presuppositional apologist seeks to argue from the inside to out. What is meant by this is that the presuppositional apologist will not try to find common logical ground that could be agreed upon by the

9. Gundry and Cowen, *Five Views*, 15.

opposition, and in this case, the Muslim party. This is because, at the heart of the matter for presupposition apologists, the opposition is at odds with God and favors their rebellious status.

As Beilby writes,

> According to the presuppositionalist, the problem with the non-Christian is not a lack of good reasons, but innate sinfulness manifested as a rebellion against God, a rebellion that first and foremost amounts to a refusal to acknowledge God's proper place. Consequently, the authority of Scripture and of Jesus Christ must be presupposed before a sense can be made of arguments for the truthfulness of Christianity. Presuppositionalism is, therefore sometimes labeled a "no-step" apologetic approach, for there are no argumentative steps that lead directly to the conclusion of the truthfulness of Christianity.[10]

For instance, this study is directed to respond to the Muslim theory that Jesus survived the cross. The presuppositions that separate the Christians and Muslims do not allow for commonality for this discussion. Simply put, Christians and Muslims have different worldviews and different ways on how they cope with how the world is. Therefore, on matters of salvation and the cross, they will not or cannot agree.

Since this is the case, the overall strategy of a presuppositionalist for this conversation would be to appeal to the opposition by utilizing the original authority of Scripture. However, this presents a problem since the opposition does not agree with the views of salvation, sin, and the Triune God. The authority of Scripture makes sense to a believer of Christ but not to a non-believer. For the Christian, it is reasonable that God is the judge and sin must be judged, as humanity is tainted with sin makes us unworthy and guilty. The Christian also understands that prayer and sacrificing the blood of animals was only temporary, and that humanity was still under the wrath of God's judgment. Therefore, God loved the

---

10. Beilby, "Varieties of Apologetics," 33.

world that He gave his Son as the ultimate sacrifice for all who would believe in him (John 3:16).

The Muslim who does not acknowledge that the sins of Adam were passed down through his bloodline, but that every human is responsible for the keeping of purity until they sin (refer to previous chapters for reference). This is not to state that the presuppositionalist is ineffective in this conversation of the cross, but it is to state that other apologetical approaches would serve this scenario. Weathers notes: "Presuppositionalism, as it has come to be known, advances that any true knowledge of God is impossible outside the Bible."[11] Furthermore, the presuppositional apologist's argument is very important.

The case for presuppositionalism would only revolve around Scripture. Following such, the argument would more than likely reflect the absence of righteousness of humanity, highlight the mercy, judgment, and love of God through Christ, and conclude that the only to way live in this world is to abandon the desires of the flesh and sinful thinking to follow Christ.

This conclusion highlights several truths: 1. People, in their rationality and presumptions outside of Scripture, are flawed at best; therefore, all efforts on what is moral become misguided without God. 2. Humanity would choose not God, not Christ, and not righteousness, so God in His love and mercy gave us His Son and offered eternal life for those who would believe. 3. After accepting Christ, the individual would also accept that he is not worthy to receive mercy and salvation, but also accept that he desperately needs it. Without these presuppositions, the conversation from this perspective is lost.

Presuppositionalism focuses primarily on the linear approach as Habermas stated, rather than circular: God's rationality → human faith → human reasoning.[12] While some do not agree with this assessment, this study took a more evidential/classical approach to this problem of the crucifixion. To answer whether Jesus would survive the cross from a medical perspective would be

11. Weathers, "Gordon Haddon Clark," 500.

12. Frame, "Presuppositional Apologist's," 354.

difficult to incorporate the presuppositional argument as a base. Rather, an argument from evidence would be best used because from medical rationality, the opposition and those of the Christian faith could come to similar logical conclusions.

Supernatural Revelation

Revelation means revealing something unknown to either an individual or a group of people. To have a revelation, a person probably experiences something similar to an awakening of some sort, while gaining clarity on what was revealed. The supernatural is something not of this realm, the unseen, and often misunderstood by some. This unseen realm or heavenly realm is the area in which the throne of God resides, according to the book of Revelation.

To receive a supernatural revelation, it would have to come from a source outside the natural realm. Christians believe that God gives revelation to those who seek him, and it is through the work of the Holy Spirit that man can have clarity when studying Scripture. The hermeneutical process involves the Holy Spirit. The Bible tells readers that the essential prerequisite for understanding the things of God is having the Spirit of God (1 Cor 2:11) and that the Christians, having received the anointing of the Spirit, do not even need a teacher (1 John 2:27).[13]

Presuppositionalists believe that through this special supernatural revelation, the person who is hearing the Gospel would be able to follow the presuppositions of Christianity. One of the first presuppositions of Christianity is to accept that no one is righteous, and because no one is righteous, humanity is all guilty under the judgment of God. Therefore, a savior is necessary for humanity because no being can stand before the judgment of God. No angel or human. The second presupposition that needs to be accepted is that through the cross, through Christ Jesus, the world was saved and justified.

13. Silva, "Who Needs Hermeneutics," 18.

If these two cannot be agreed upon, then the conversation could not go any further. However, to understand the Bible, to believe in the Gospel, God would have to reveal himself to that person who is earnestly searching for him. This would be covered under special revelation.

Ryrie remarks:

> Undebatable is the incarnation of Jesus Christ was a major avenue of special revelation. He exegeted the Father (John 1:14), revealing the nature of God (14:9), the power of God (3:2), the wisdom of God (7:46), the glory of God (1:14), the life of God (1 John 1:1–3), and the love of God (Rom 5:8). Our Lord did all this by both His acts (John 2:11) and His words (Matt 16:17).[14]

Furthermore, while science and the laws of logic are indeed important pieces of information that govern how the world functions, apart from God there is no reliable basis for entertaining either, because God is the foundation of all things.[15]

Further discussion from the presuppositionalist would be helpful once the person realizes that without God, without Christ, without the crucifixion, all is lost. However, in terms of this topic of the cross, it becomes rather difficult to continue this discussion from a medical perspective. Therefore, the evidentialist apologist would more than likely offer a clearer argument for this particular subject.

Evidentialist Apologetics

Gary Habermas believes that the evidential method of apologetics has much in common with the classical method, with the chief difference being the way in which historical evidences are used.[16] Much like the classical approach, evidentialists utilize resources at their disposal to prove that the Bible is very much correct in its

14. Ryrie, *Basic Theology*, 73.

15. Reymond, *New Systematic Theology*, 146.

16. Habermas, "Evidential Apologetics," 92.

truth propositions. This by no means suggests that evidentialists do not trust in the Bible; instead, they are merely attempting to defend what Scripture states through means of logic and historical data for those who will not accept, or do not trust the authority of Scripture.

At the core of Christian evidentialism is the Gospel and all its accounts, therein. Many strides in historical data mining were made to help bolster many of the arguments from an apologetical sense. Archaeologists have found evidence of the shroud of Jesus, as mentioned in the previous chapter. Historians have found evidence of a historical Jesus, the lives of the apostles, and so on. As for the topic of this book, evidence was provided from different fields of study to converge on one point; the point that Jesus would not survive a Roman crucifixion. This included information as how historically a crucifixion would take place, the tools at their disposal, the area and timing of the event, and the records from the eyewitnesses corroborating what was found when archaeologist piece artifacts together become invaluable for a historian and evidentialist.

The Argument

The argument from an evidentialist perspective would include historical data founded by Christian archaeologists and secular archaeologists. If the truth is founded, backed by the tools and criteria of history, then the evidence presented becomes valid. However, there are some who believe that history could disprove the Bible, but God has affirmed His word throughout the foundations of the world. Therefore, what would be found while discovering historical facts would only bolster the truth propositions that the Bible asserts. The evidentialist treats one or more historical arguments as being able both to indicate God's existence and activity and to indicate which variety of theism is true.[17]

17. Habermas, "Evidential Apologetics," 92.

For instance, when discussing on the crucifixion of Jesus, there is historical data that backs up the truthfulness of the Scripture. This same data was not only presented by supporters of Christianity but also non-supporters. The benefit of having data from non-interested party members signifies that the information is non-bias. The evidentialist will review all of the data and what is generally accepted will be pursued. Generally, historians will agree on theories that are supported by substantial findings, then these theories will lead to plausible conclusions. The crucifixion of Jesus is no different. Many documents and artifacts lead to the conclusion that Jesus was crucified, and that same data support the conclusion that Jesus was dead, moreover, the fact remains that no one survived a Roman crucifixion.

Since the non-supporters of Christianity present historical evidence that falls in line with what Scripture states, the logical approach would be to trust what Scripture asserts about the events of the cross. Peter Schäfer, in his review of Jesus in the Talmud, is very clear on how the Jewish authorities felt and said about Jesus and his death, which is stated in the previous chapter. It is important to mention that the historical data is only supporting what the Bible affirms, and not replacing the authority of Scripture.

Therefore, as it stands the crucifixion of Jesus Christ historically happened during the time when Pilate governed Jerusalem. From there, information would be extracted as to the fashion of how the Romans punished their citizens, criminals, and people under their control. There were rules for how Romans were punished as opposed to other groups of people. This was known through how Paul was treated as a Roman citizen, and the treatment he received when he announced his citizenship before the Jews executed their judgment in the book of Acts. This treatment was not afforded to Jesus who was a Jew. History tells about the horrors of how people were executed by the Romans.

Although the Bible is almost the first place many would come to know about the crucifixion, historically, the Romans did not invent it; rather, they improved on it. History also plays into how someone would be medically treated if they suffered injuries.

However, in that specific time, the injuries that Jesus suffered before being hung on the cross and his time on the cross, all point to no known recovery by conventional early-century medical standards. Although herbs and some topical solutions were used to treat some wounds, the kind of injuries that Jesus suffered would require more than what that century had to offer.

The realm of medicine has indeed evolved to where it is now. Presently a pig's heart could be utilized in a heart transplant, temporarily.[18] Blood drives are normalized throughout the United States and even afforded to its military. Pain could be lessened quickly by injecting the medicine directly into the muscle, but the syringe design was not developed in the time of Jesus. A blood transfusion was not developed during the time of the Romans, and neither was transplanting a possibility. Of course, if the possibility of these medical advancements were accessible during that time, then the theory of Jesus surviving the cross would be worth pursuing, and Deedat's line of thinking would have some validity. However, historically, this is not the case and does not line with the evidence that was preserved throughout time.

Adding to the argument from the evidentialist point of view would be the authority and trustworthiness of Scripture because the Bible, specifically, the Gospels talks more about Jesus than other ancient and religious works. Also, the Bible is also considered a historical book that cannot be overlooked while talking about a Roman crucifixion. The Bible should be considered one piece of evidence that God has preserved throughout the course of time.

TRUSTWORTHINESS OF SCRIPTURE FOR HISTORIANS

When viewing the Bible (from the Old Testament to the New), there are multiple times where a historian can figure the time and place of the events therein. The naming of kings, the battles, the locations, and other interesting facts are all throughout the Bible.

---

18. Pierson, "Pig-to-human Heart," 2672.

This information helps apologist and others understand from a natural sense that the Bible is not simply a religious book, but a book of historical information. Therefore, when talking about the crucifixion of Jesus, specifically if Jesus survived the ordeal, the validity of the writers of the Gospels brings an intriguing argument within itself.

Earlier in another chapter, it was stated that historians typically agree on these minimal facts. Jesus was crucified, Jesus was dead, and then Jesus was later seen. If Christ survived the cross, it would explain why Jesus was seen later, but would not explain why the disciples would die for a lie not simply die but be hunted down and die in a gruesome way. This is not similar to having someone give their life in a kamikaze attack for their faith and beliefs. The disciples died for believing in the risen Savior and did not once recant their story. The difference between one dying for the beliefs of ISIS and a martyr is substantial.

For instance, before the Gospels were written, oral tradition was the norm due to how it was in their culture. So, when the story of Jesus was told, it was broadcasted by people who knew Jesus (disciples and apostles) and corroborated by eyewitnesses. "Their recollections were not individual memories but *collective* ones— confirmed by other eyewitnesses and burned into their minds by the constant retelling of the story. *Memory in the community* is a death blow to the view that the disciples simply forgot the real Jesus."[19]

Therefore, the Gospels, out of response to time and the second coming of the Lord, more than likely wrote the Gospels out of necessity. Moreover, the Gospels were written during the time of those same eyewitnesses within four decades of the crucifixion of Jesus. The likelihood of false doctrine being so widespread during that time becomes unlikely. These same sharers of the Gospel would then be captured and killed in horrid fashions. If Jesus was a lie, Paul who was known for helping capture Christians and then converted to Christianity a short time later is difficult to contend with.

19. Komoszewski, *Reinventing Jesus*, 33–34.

The Gospels all tell the same story of Jesus, and though it may be in a different order, the order is relatively small. The life of Jesus was preserved in these writings and because of the accuracy of the historical events recorded, scholars can trace much of the story from this era. Generally, when it comes to the life of Jesus, the disconnection of what is fact or believed stems from when the direction of the discussion includes his divinity.

A prime example of this was mentioned when Timothy of Bagdad had an intriguing conservation about the Trinity with the Caliph. The Caliphs hold true to the Quran, and obviously have reservations about the deity of Christ, the Trinity, and how Christians revere Christ. Edward Smither and Trevor Castor recount this apologetical discussion between the two in this article, and the section on the death of Jesus lays a logical argument. Timothy continues the dialogue by appealing to Old Testament prophecies about the Messiah dying by crucifixion (Ps 22; Zech 13:7; Isa 53:5; Dan 9:26).[20]

Timothy engages this point of the conversation by using the Quran and the Scriptures to build his case. The evidence in the Quran, the Bible, and what the history of the Jews did to their prophets led Timothy to conclude that Jesus died on the cross. Regardless of how a person would feel about what God could have done or should have done, it does not change the fact that God did not change his mission for redeeming the world. The evidentialist pulls from many avenues of information and defend their faith with what is gained in their search.

The embarrassing moments recorded in the Gospels also help with the truthfulness of the crucifixion.[21] This criterion is important because it does not dress Jesus up as a type of superhero. Rather, it shows a kind of weakness and peace in one who told about future events, showing miracle-working power, and could have easily dispatched his arrestors. Jesus would later be subjected to the Roman justice system and ways that were not hospitable in the slightest. All that the Romans did to Jesus reduced any chance

20. Smither and Castor, "Timothy I of Bagdad," 205.

21. Licona, *Resurrection of Jesus*, 306.

of surviving the cross drastically if there would be one. Moreover, even if Jesus had been removed from his cross prematurely and medically assisted, his chances of survival were quite bleak. In addition, no evidence exists that Jesus was removed while alive or that he was provided any medical care whatsoever, much less Rome's best.[22]

APOLOGETIC RESPONSE

This chapter reviewed some of the apologetical approaches to the crucifixion, and all arrived at the same conclusion. Jesus did die on the cross. They all arrived at this deduction not only because at heart they are Christians, but because it is the most rational analysis. First, Jesus was charged under Roman law, and being a Jew did not benefit Jesus's position. The Romans would crush any sign of rebellion, and Jesus would have been seen as the leader of said rebellion.

Second, Jesus experienced brutal treatment before the cross that was known to kill some before even reaching the cross. Jesus was beaten, muscles ripped, bleeding, blunt force trauma, and all of this before picking up his cross to be carried to the final spot for execution. Last, the medical attention that Jesus would have needed to survive the cross was not developed in that era for Jesus to be seen just only three days afterward. Furthermore, Jesus was able to eat, walk, and function normally as if nothing happened, which points to his resurrection.

These facts lead to the most probable and logical conclusion that Jesus died on the cross. The spear to the side of Jesus arrives after the Roman soldier announces that Jesus was already dead. The medical analysis of blood and water coming out was due to Jesus already being dead and more than likely the result of blunt force trauma. The spear did not suddenly revive Jesus as Deedat believes, and historically, would have still required Jesus to be hospitalized for months. All the evidence from historical documents

22. Licona, *Resurrection of Jesus*, 311.

and medical suggestions steer to the conclusion that Jesus did die on the cross.

Although the opposition believes that Jesus escaped the clutches of the Romans, what is agreed upon by many scholars is several facts, or minimal facts, that determine the historicity of the crucifixion of Jesus. The numerous sources that attest to the trustworthiness of what Scripture stated about Jesus dying on the cross, the brutal process of the crucifixion, which was designed to kill, and very early testimonies of Jesus dying on the cross all attribute to the historicity of the story of the crucifixion.[23] "The history of the apostles corroborates the truth of Christianity. The dramatic change in the attitude of the apostles—from fear and dismay to boldness and confidence—shows the truth of Jesus's resurrection and his continuing presence among them."[24]

Considering all of this information, a few things are very apparent. One, Jesus was crucified by the Romans. Two, the Roman crucifixion was never halted during Jesus's time on the cross. Three, the crucifixion was designed to kill their victims. Fourth, the design of a crucifixion required more medical attention to an individual than that era could receive. Finally, Jesus was believed to be dead by all that knew and cared and did not care for his well-being. If Jesus would have survived the cross and was able to be fully functional in three days would be a medical phenomenon, if it would not be for the multiple sources that agree that Jesus was dead. With all this information, it should be concluded that the assertions made by Deedat do not follow a logical or scientific pattern.

The logical approach would be to include God's justice, which is pure, holy, and righteous. Justice continues to serve the interests of peace, with equity and mercy being important components of the concept of justice, rather than being opposed to it.[25] Therefore, to keep the peace, to settle what is right, and show mercy, Christ must be crucified. Without this, man will be accused by Satan, and

23. Beck and Shaw, "Gary R. Habermas," 773–74.
24. Mcclymond, "Jonathan Edwards," 333.
25. Vidu, *Atonement, Law, and Justice*, 14.

risk being judged under the full weight of the Majesty of God. God must respond to sin, and with Christ as man's advocate, humanity can be forgiven for their trespasses. Repentance is mentioned throughout the Old and New Testament, but without the cross, the attempt to repent is in short sighted.

Repentance, according to Christian thought, involves the work of the Holy Spirit to change the person. However, if Jesus survived the cross, then the Holy Spirit did not come as well (John 14:26; John 16:7). These passages both talk about the Holy Spirit, but specifically in John 16:7 when Jesus tells his disciples that he must go away for the Holy Spirit to come unto them. The cross is detrimental to Satan's plan for humanity, and beneficial for those who would believe in Christ. Therefore, it is without a doubt that Christ crucified is necessary for salvation.

From a medical stance, though there have been many people who have survived traumatic experiences, those same had was afforded the opportunity to this era's scientific advancements. The timing of Jesus's death and the witnesses account of seeing him later would not allow for this to be possible from a medical perspective. However, if the argument shifted to the fact that Jesus survived the cross because of the will of God, then there would be a more severe problem. Jesus himself told his disciples of his death before it happened, and from the Muslim community, Jesus is a prophet of God. Jesus cannot be a prophet of God and false. Furthermore, if the New Testament account is readily accepted, then the Old Testament would suffice.

The prophet Isaiah stated in chapter 53 that it pleased the Father, being Yahweh, to bruise him. The other prophecies concerning Jesus about his bones not being broken, which during the crucifixion process was the norm. However, because of prophecy, this did not happen. The prophets told things about Jesus before his time, and all went according to the will of God. Furthermore, what is not found in Scripture is God telling Jesus that he would not allow him to be crucified. Jesus while praying in the garden cried out before God to remove the burden, but stated that God's will shall be done, meaning that Jesus would be crucified.

Finally, going back to the medical conditions mentioned in the earlier chapter, the damage to the hemothorax, asphyxiation, loss of blood, and hematidrosis all factor in some of the leading causes for Jesus's death on the cross. Jesus would need access to the best treatment available, however, it is not documented or witnesses by any source that this type was available for Jesus. Jesus was sentenced to death by Rome, but before Rome was involved, the Jewish religious leaders sought to deal with Jesus according to Mark 14:1. The tools required to help Jesus recover in just three days' time would have to be administered in the best ideal location. However, Jesus was in the tomb, locked away, and guarded by Roman soldiers because the Jewish leadership believed the disciples would steal the body.

The only logical conclusion to this ordeal is that it is not medically feasible for Jesus to survive a Roman crucifixion, and this conclusion follows from what is historically known. Therefore, it is further concluded that Scripture is correct in what it affirms about Jesus of Nazareth—that he died on the cross, and then later rose on the third day.

5

Evidentialist Appraisal

For Christians, the crucifixion and resurrection of Jesus Christ are quintessential subjects—Jesus died on the cross and rose on the third day. The doctrine of Christianity hangs on the fact that Jesus Christ died on the cross and rose on the third day. After his resurrection, Jesus is on the throne forever more seated on the right side of the Father, and when he comes back every knee will bow, and every tongue will confess that Jesus Christ is Lord (Phil 2:10, John 13:13, Rom 14:9). The life, ministry, and supremacy of Jesus Christ should be a joy and recognized as a need for the entire world. Ironically, this discussion does not just stop with those of the Christian faith; other religions, and schools of thought have discussed the impact of Jesus Christ on the world.

Unfortunately, even after reading about the life of Jesus, and all that he has done, and promised to do in the coming age, there are some who choose not to believe in the biblical, traditional story of Jesus Christ. These skeptics have developed heterodox theories concerning the crucifixion, which warrant a response. Their interpretation, whether it be based on genuine unfamiliarity or a lack of belief in who Jesus is, cries out for correction.

This study seeks to help guide those towards the truth of Scripture—that Jesus physically died on the cross and miraculously arose just three days afterward. Therefore, to cover the circumstances surrounding the events of the crucifixion, observing what is medically plausible, and observing what is historically recorded, this study will shed more light on the truth propositions that Scripture asserts.

The aforementioned skeptics in earlier chapters (such as Swoon Theorists Deedat, Ally, and their followers) do not believe that the story of Jesus's crucifixion is essentially factual. Essentially, Christians, Muslims, Jewish, or atheism, all claim to search after truth. However, in Christianity, the truth is that the crucifixion and resurrection of Jesus are extraordinary. Moreover, there is evidence to support that this controversial event truly did happen, and only adds to the awe effect it has on many people. This is understandable because who could believe such an incredible story without evidence? So, looking at the apologetic response to these concerns will help many understand the position of this study.

PROOF OF EVIDENCE

This book proposes that Jesus did indeed die on the cross and that it was medically impossible for Jesus (or any other human during that time) to survive a crucifixion. The apologetic response requires special attention to evidence that stems from historical pieces of evidence that are surrounded by what Scripture presuppositionally states, and in turn, this is utilized to help point to the truth.

The skeptic's charge is that Jesus survived the cross; however, historically, there are accounts from believers and non-believers who acknowledge that Jesus did, in fact, die on the cross. The Talmud records that Jesus was killed, and this comes from writers who did not view Jesus as the promised Messiah to come.

In the study of the empty tomb, historians did not dispute whether Jesus was dead; rather, the location of the tomb where he was buried was questioned. Therefore, as it stands for many scholars, Jesus did die, but regardless of what some scholars have agreed upon, the charge from the people who developed and agree with the Swoon theory, is that Jesus was alive while being taken down from the cross, and he hid in the tomb for three days, to later appear to his disciples as promised.

The skeptics do seem to have a point; in the Gospels, there was no mention of a physician that verified that Jesus was dead. Despite what seems like a worthy attempt to justify their position on this matter, there is a flaw to this line of thinking. The Swoon Theory proposes that since no medical personnel verified that Jesus was actually dead, the possibility of survival is signified. Others who support the Swoon Theory (like the Ahmadiyya Muslim group) affirm that Jesus escaped death and traveled to India to continue his work of preaching to the lost sheep of Israel located there.[1]

Moreover, Zafar Harris claims that in Islam, Jesus is considered as the Messiah and last prophet of Israel and did not die on the cross. However, he further states that Jesus was birthed by the virgin Mary, and his coming was foretold to be the Messiah of the Israelites, and Harris also states that because the kingdom of Israel was split and many were exiled, Jesus's mission was not completed on the cross because he only stayed in the lands of Judea.[2]

Harris believes that the crucifixion of Jesus Christ is important, but he also has an entire section dedicated to several theories about the crucifixion. Special attention was given to the survival theory because Jesus's body was given to his disciple, Joseph of Arimathea, according to Matthew 27:37. Harris believes that this was a mistake made by Pilate because it allowed Jesus to escape and did not explain how blood and water can flow out of a supposed dead man.[3] He believes that Nicodemus was physician who helped Jesus heal up with the mixtures of myrrh and aloe because the Gospel of John provides the amount that he brought with him. However, it is important to note that the thought of Nicodemus being a physician is not recognized in most other circles. Much of Harris's theory ultimately promotes that Jesus was only a prophet

1. Embrayil, *Jesus' Life in India*, 10.

2. Zafar, *Demystifying* Islam, 147–48.

3. Zafar, *Demystifying* Islam, 161.

for Israel and their Messiah, but not the Son of God as Christianity claims.

Supporters of the Swoon theory and the Ahmadiyya receive much of their information about Jesus from various Gospels from the Christian Bible, the Gospel of Thomas, from what the Quran teaches, and from some thoughts from notable authors from their community. What an evidentialist would do is observe the evidence provided concerning what a person goes through while being crucified. The question that naysayers and Christians should consider is whether it is more plausible for someone to survive the ordeal, and what would it take to survive?

The problem is that there are some who have been noted to survive trauma like being shot multiple times, but this is not a true assessment of the issue presented here. In order for those trauma patients to survive, they would have to have sought medical treatment and an extended recovery time. The criticism from Swoon theorists does not eliminate the flogging, the loss of blood, the spear to the side, and the traumatic experience Jesus went through while on the cross. Therefore, the problem that Swoon Theorists must acknowledge is that the report state Jesus was seen just three days after being taken down from the cross and then buried. The evidence seems consistent with what Scripture recorded.

The goal of evidential apologetics is to highlight the evidence presented in the Bible from a historical aspect. This is extremely helpful as a guide towards understanding truth propositions that the Bible produces, but what evidential apologists cannot do is truly prove miracle claims. The reason being is that from the position of history, a historian can only verify what was recorded.

For instance, it is accepted by most scholars that Jesus was a real person. There are tools at the historian's disposal that are used to verify the authenticity of historical topics. Scripture tells that during the reign of Caesar Augustus Jesus was born in Luke 2:1, and the gospel of Matthew tells of Herod. "Luke relates a census 'while Quirinius was governor'" that he fits into the same time period as John's birth and that sent Joseph and Mary to Bethlehem.

Instructed by a dream, the family goes to Egypt to escape pending danger.

Finally, after the slaughter of children two years and younger by Herod, Matthew 2:19–20 notes that Joseph was instructed in a dream to bring back Jesus and Mary from Egypt. The call to return followed Herod's death. Thus, in different ways, Luke and Matthew show agreement about the general timing of Jesus's birth within the latter part of Herod the Great's reign.[4]

Therefore, to see which Herod Matthew was referring to, historians would determine which Herod was installed in Jerusalem during the reign of Caesar Augustus and during the time of Pilate. The evidence found historically during the reign of those individuals would help point to the reality that Jesus was born during that time but would not truly prove of the miracle virgin birth, only guide the researcher to the trustworthiness of the Bible. Furthermore, it is the goal of a Christian apologist that the person they are discussing biblical facts with would make the decision to come to the Christian faith.

It is worth explaining historically what a crucifixion is. The word, crucifixion, is synonymous with words like execution, punishment, torment, agony, and suffering, according to the English language. In Greek, the word, crucify, is translated to *stauròō* taken from the word, *staurŏs*. These words mean to impale on the cross, to extinguish, to subdue, and crucify. From here, identifying the type of crucifixion Jesus Christ went through was not something to be taken lightly. People who were crucified went through intense pain, and agony and were placed there to be eliminated. Therefore, it could safely be asserted that the goal of crucifixion, as the Bible mentions was to remove the possibility of survival. They also broke the legs of their victims to quicken the execution, but it is recorded in the Gospels that Jesus did not have his legs broken. In fact, he was pronounced dead before they pierced his side, according to John 19:33–34.

Of course, someone could interpret that the crucifixion had multiple meanings, with one meaning death and one just meaning

4. Bock, *Studying the Historical Jesus*, 69.

punishment, and we will cover both of those circumstances in this book. However, to be clear on the position of this book, it is believed and understood that when Scripture utilizes the word crucify it is not interchangeable with punishment as a parent would punish their child. This is not the kind of punishment which Scripture and history describe. It was not like, "Hey Jesus, you served your time on the cross. You have some bruises, and you should be rehabilitated now. You are free to go, and do not do this again."

It would be something if something like this happened. Christians would have to throw away crosses hanging on the wall. They would have to apologize for all the confrontations they had in Jesus's name and would have a difficult time explaining all who were martyred for preaching Christ crucified.

Presuppositional Apologetics

Christ crucified has been debated by many scholars like Gary Habermas, William Lane Craig, and Michael Licona. They seem to take the evidential apologetical approach to guide people towards biblical truths about the death and resurrection of Jesus Christ. Despite the evidence that they all have brought to the conversation, skeptics still question the reliability of the Gospels and, more importantly, Jesus Christ. Now the classical method of apologetics is about the same as the evidential, both dealing with historical evidence, while presuppositional apologetics believes that the Christian faith is the only rational and logical basis of thought.

Therefore, in presuppositional apologetics, the goal is to point out inconsistencies within other worldviews. The main worldview that this study argues against is the view presented by the Muslim party and Swoon theorists. Discussing ideas with others from different worldviews will most of the time present some difficulty. Essentially, Christians are asking individuals who do not believe or view the world how they view the world, but that does not translate to well.

So, why would they not believe in Jesus Christ as the Son of God, the one who died on the cross, the one who sacrificed himself, and the one who God sent because He loved the world? Finally, what would it be the outcome and benefit of being right if Jesus never was crucified? The answer could lie in their worldview. As it stands, the worldview of a Muslim suggests that their way is the only way to properly serve God. Islam teaches that each person is born in a state of spiritual purity, but upbringing and the allure of worldly pleasures may corrupt us.

Nonetheless, sins are not inherited and, for that matter, not even Adam and Eve will be punished for their sins, for God has forgiven them;[5] therefore, there is no need for a redeemer. Furthermore, their views concerning salvation are that each person is responsible for their own salvation, which negates the Christian doctrine of salvation, and the need for the Messiah to come and save the world through his redemptive blood.[6]

The outcome that undoubtedly follows is that without Jesus, they could present to the world something that makes sense to them in terms of faith, hope, and servitude to Allah. This is how the Muslims view the world, how they cope with how the world functions, and how they rationalize their understanding of life itself. Without this understanding, the world as they perceive it would crumble. Their faith in what the Quran teaches guides them towards some peace, and some measure of stability. Furthermore, according to the Muslim faith, Christ not being crucified and resurrected means that God is impersonal. There does not appear to be an issue within the Muslim community of an impersonal God because God is far above lowly humans, so it fits their logic.

What is alarming is that God's love is truly unknown, and salvation is not certain, because there is no Christ, no Lamb to ransom the people for God. The Muslim way into eternity would be met by prayer and whether God deems them worthy. This sounds fair and righteous; however, the problem of uncertainty without Christ is illuminated in Christian doctrine. The Christian worldview acknowledges that no matter many times a person prays to

---

5. Andrews, *Is the Quran*, 42–43.
6. Andrews, *Is the Quran*, 44–46.

God, without Jesus Christ, their position is one like that of a thief because humanity still remains damnably guilty.

Both Christian and Muslim faiths both admit that all mankind came through Adam. Therefore, we are all the seed of Adam, and that through Adam's actions, humanity's blood became tainted with sin. Christianity believes that humanity is not worthy due to our attraction to sin. No matter how many times someone has prayed, sacrificed, and desired not to displease God, the fact is there is no life without Christ. Previously, humanity would have to sacrifice animals to appease the blood debt required for sin; however, this was only temporary and ineffective to the overall weight of sin. No human could appease this debt.

Consider the following: if someone needed a blood transfusion, and the person donating the blood was impure, the person receiving the blood would still remain sick. That person would need a transfusion from an outside source, from one who was not tainted. Since Jesus never came from the line of Adam, he was never tainted by sin. The book of Hebrews explains this concept and signifies the world's need for Jesus Christ.

Another possible reason for the Muslim faith not readily accepting Jesus Christ as Lord and Savior is likely the fact that the cross confounds even the wise. In 1 Corinthians 1:20–25, Paul wrote that the crucified Christ is above the wisdom of the Greeks and displeasure to Jews. A crucified Christ meant that God redeemed the world through the lamb, one who did not deserve death, one who was without sin, and one who would fulfill the Davidic promise as king and high priest forever.

The cross can confound the wise for several reasons. One would be the law written in Deuteronomy 21:23 decreeing that anyone who is hung on a tree is under God's curse. The question that follows is how is a supposed cursed man the Savior? Verse 22 reminds the reader that the man must be found guilty. Jesus was not guilty; Jesus did not commit any crime on earth or by heaven's account.

The second reason why the Cross confuses the wise is probably that some believe that God should not hold humanity accountable for something that happened many thousands of years ago in Eden. In other words, how could a good, just, and righteous God hold man accountable for something that Adam did? Then how could one man provide the cure for the problem? The Apostle Paul answers the first part of this question in Romans 9:19 when this question was asked again. The response reminds humanity of God's sovereignty, authority, and power, and how God chose to save mankind instead of his wrath. God chose patience instead of destruction. Paul also reminds humanity of whom they are compared to God.

IMPORTANCE OF THIS RESEARCH

This research will not be the first of its kind to defend what Scripture says about Jesus Christ to be true. Licona dealt with the resurrection of Jesus from a historical point of view. He wanted to approach the resurrection story under the same guidelines as a historian to help signify the plausibility of the story. In such research, it was found, under these same guidelines, that Jesus was seen after he was reported dead. However, the guidelines never attempted to prove any happenings of a miracle. Although some would admit that historically Jesus was known to be dead and then later was seen later, this undoubtedly points to the miracle.

Habermas also has done exhaustive work in the study of the resurrection of Jesus Christ. What is noticed here is that much work has gone into the resurrection aspect while touching on the crucifixion. The problem mentioned in the previous chapters was that the argument used to deny the resurrection of Jesus Christ mainly focused on the crucifixion to eliminate the possibility of returning from the dead. If Jesus never was dead, then the resurrection never took place. This study focuses mainly on the crucifixion, as to help further understanding of what was possible, and what would have normally taken place, and to promote that Jesus actually died on the cross.

There are substantiating reasons for this theory, one being the way Jesus was flogged before ever going to the cross. The issue of blood and water flowing after being pierced in the side was another indicator that something even more troubling in the crucifixion story. The very fact that Roman soldiers were superb in how they tortured and killed people. Not that this is a good thing, just that they were very efficient at what they did in that regard.

Also, among the other reasons for crucifixion being utilized, execution and not just humiliation was one of the reasons. While this study has not gone into depth as to why Jesus was such a problem for the Roman government; however, it will be mentioned because legally the Roman government had the authority to issue capital punishment in that region. The Jews, on the other hand, did not have the authority to crucify their criminals according to John 18:31.

As mentioned earlier, talking about the crucifixion and resurrection of Jesus Christ is nothing new. Christians, atheists, Muslims, and other various faith groups talk about this subject. How could we add more to this well-studied subject? The answer lies within the medical side of things instead of purely theology. From what is understood in this century about how one processes stress, the effects of stress on the mind and body, the information on blood loss, the information on trauma victims, and simply how the body function is incredible. However, medical science does not claim to understand all of the body; there are some matters that they are certain about concerning the body.

Scientists understand how asphyxiation works. They have a general understanding of what happens to people during blood loss. As time went on, the general understanding of medicine increased. Therefore, certain things that were considered medical phenomena could be explained more clearly in this century. This is important to mention because while inspecting the comments made by individuals like Deedat and the ideas from the Ahmadiyya, members claim that a dead body within a few hours would not pour out blood and water, but according to Meyer, the most common cause of hemothorax is trauma and is located in the chest area.[7]

7. Meyer, "Hemothorax Related to Trauma," 48.

Also, Broderick concurs with this assessment and states, "Thoracic trauma continues to be a substantial cause of morbidity and mortality. Chest injuries occur in approximately 60% of multitrauma patients and are responsible for 20% to 25% of trauma-related mortalities."[8] A patient with hemothorax would more than likely have gone through blunt or penetrating thoracic trauma. The very fluid in the person's body becomes separated between the heavier blood cells and plasma cells, which is a common trait and could medically explain the blood and water scene from the cross.

Jesus was flogged, which means beaten by Roman tools of torture. The whips were not the same whips that are utilized on horses with chariots to enable them to go faster. These Roman flagellums were typically constructed of a wooden handle and have several leather straps with metal, glass, or bone tied into the straps.[9] Jesus would have been beaten from his to his buttocks, flesh, and meat would have been ripped from his body, and this was only the starting point for their methods of torture. Therefore, by the time of being pierced in his side by the Roman guard, it would not have revived him; instead, due to all the scrouge Jesus went through, and the cross itself, it is medically plausible that he died in the hour that the Gospels mention. The blood and water flowing are not a result of one being alive but of one who has expired from trauma.

PLAUSIBLE REASONS FOR DEATH

The authors of the Bible recorded the events of the crucifixion to share how the Lord died. The story is gruesome and heartfelt and gives information as to how the Roman government issued their methods of capital punishment. The question is, how did Jesus die so quickly while others were recorded to spend days on the cross? Unfolding this question will require a bit of forensic work to narrow down what was plausible or not. Therefore, it would be more practical to start this investigation in the garden when Jesus

8. Broderick, "Hemothorax," 23.
9. Borchert, *John 12–21*.

was praying. Mark 14:34–38 talks about Jesus being in sorrow for what was about to happen, and Luke 22:44 tells that Jesus was in agony and that his sweat became like great drops of blood falling to the ground. Why would Luke talk about Jesus's sweat? Since Luke's occupation was a physician, he is more than likely connecting to what resonates with him, as others have done when retelling a story.

According to Michael Licona, historians ancient and modern alike are selective in the material they report.[10] So, Luke (in this case) noticed something interesting when talking about how Jesus was sweating. Sweating big drops of blood has been known to be associated with a medical condition called hermatidrosis. This condition is rare, and it was confirmed during the twentieth century.[11]

At that time, it was able to be treated properly, but during Jesus's time, there is no record of Jesus receiving treatment for this, though this condition is not serious, it may contribute to a person feeling dehydrated. Furthermore, this condition was associated with people who were under emotional stress or physical stress.[12] Both of the Gospels mentioned above attest to the stress, anguish, and sorrow of Jesus while in the garden, and enough to cause Jesus to call out to God to remove the burden from him, all the while adhering to the will of God as the final say.

From the Bible, it is promoted that Jesus knew that he was going to be betrayed, sacrificed, knew that he was going to be murdered. However, knowing that it was going to happen before the time came, and knowing about it closer to the time could alter how someone may feel about a situation. Obviously, Jesus did not die in the garden with this condition, but it is important information for this forensic study. With this untreated condition, the next happenings added to the first problem. This is not to state that Jesus was a feeble and weak man. None of the synoptic gospels tell of Jesus being sick during his ministry, nor during the brief moments

10. Licona, *Resurrection of Jesus*, 32.
11. Bhattacharya, "Hematidrosis," 703–4.
12. Bhattacharya, "Hematidrosis," 703–4.

of adolescents recorded in Luke. However, this time was different. This time Jesus was on the path of sacrifice, to show that he is the Lamb of God. Furthermore, Jesus who is fully man and fully God could sweat blood and still remain the King, and the one who was, who is, and who is to come.

This condition is not connected to Jesus alone, but there were cases of this rare condition reported in 2020. On August 3, 2020, Ryo Matsuoka reported that hematidrosis is more common in people from Asia, especially in India and Pakistan, which is around the same area where most of the biblical narratives take place.[13] Matsuoka also records the treatment utilized to help the eleven-year-old girl who had this condition for over two years. While the doctors could not establish how to rid the patient of hematidrosis, improvement was accomplished with beta-blockers or psychotropic agents like lorazepam. The conclusion was that patients with underlying psychiatric disorders showed no improvement with beta-blockers alone. Therefore, it is more likely that since Jesus did not receive medical attention for this disease, it was still a factor in how well his body was functioning after being scourged by Roman soldiers.

Roman Scourging

Scourging or flogging was described by Craig Blomberg while commentating on Matthew 27:26 as the *flagellum* that was a metal-tipped whip and the scourge itself was often fatal for most people.[14] Matthew also records that the Roman soldiers placed thorns on his head and handed him a scepter then bashed on the head, for which Blomberg stated that they used the scepter to hit Jesus on the head.[15] From what Blomberg commented, a Roman scourge was horrid; however, when observing what the Gospels describe there appears to be a problem with the commentary.

13. Matsuoka and Manabu. "Hematidrosis," 1001.
14. Blomberg, *Matthew*, 414.
15. Blomberg, *Matthew*, 415.

None of the Gospels go into detail as to which type of flogging Jesus went through. A typical Roman flogging had different meanings that should be considered when going through the Passion story of Jesus Christ. Andrea Nicolotti stated that flagellation was one of many corporal punishments that the Romans utilized.[16] Since this was one of the methods used, and the Gospels do not state which method was utilized, a brief study was conducted to verify, which was more than likely or not. There were different whips that the Romans used ranging from severe to the whips used while on chariots. Habermas referred to the Roman historian Cornelius Tacitus in his study of the *Historical Jesus* Tacitus recorded, that *Christus*, suffered the most extreme penalty during the reign of Tiberius at the hands of Pontius Pilatus, and a most mischievous superstition, which was recorded around Judea.[17]

Because Tacitus describes the treatment of Christians, named after Jesus Christ, as horrifying, there are a few things that are for certain: 1. Since Tacitus records this during the time of Pilate, the reference to the penalty refers to Christ. 2. Jesus received the most extreme castigation at the hands of the Roman government. 3. Jesus was the root of what the Romans believed was superstition, therefore, it had to be rooted out. 4. The punishments continued because the superstition rose again.

Since Tacitus was known as the greatest Roman historian, it would be safe to agree with consensus that the scourge was nothing less than with the most severe mechanisms at the executioner's disposal. Also, from Scripture in Acts 22:25–25, Paul was bound with straps so he could go through the scourge; however, because Paul was a Roman citizen, this treatment was not afforded to him. Scourging or flagellation was something to be feared during this time because of the severity of events within it. For people who went through this, they received deeps wounds down to the muscles or bones, and at times would result in death.[18] Although Jesus

---

16. Nicolotti, "*Scourge of Jesus*," 1.

17. Habermas, "Non-Christian Sources," 39.

18. Nicolotti, "*Scourge of Jesus*," 3.

did not die during the scourge, his skin and muscles were ripped by the event.

Furthermore, Jesus naturally was losing blood because of those deep wounds. The Gospel of Matthew records that during this time, after the scourge, the soldiers placed thorns on top of Jesus's head. These thorns obviously caused more blood to drip from his head. Finally, the soldiers, a battalion, mocked him while some of those there struck Jesus on the head. Whether it was with the scepter as Blomberg suggested, or with their fists or other objects, the result is that Jesus was bloody with deep wounds causing more blood loss. Losing blood can cause people to become disoriented, weak, tired, have blood pressure falling, and have shortness of breath. If Jesus was affected by any of those symptoms, being hung on the cross worsened the wounded Lamb.

The Cross

The crucifixion was an execution instituted not by the Romans. Rather, some historians trace its origins as far as the Persians; however, the Romans were known to have perfected it to what is known by reading the Gospels.[19] This barbaric form of corporate punishment included public humiliation, and dislocation of joints, making it difficult for the person to breathe, and the result would have the person in agony until they took their final breath.

In the Gospels, it is accepted by most scholars like Habermas and Boice that Jesus was nailed to the cross. However, hanging on a cross with nails, as stated in the Gospels, was debatable in some circles. Hebrew, biblical and Jewish studies lecturer Shani Berrin, while observing the Pesher Nahum Scroll from Qumran,[20] raised the question of hanging.

In terms of strangulation and being nailed to the cross because of the search for a medical cause of death, there was a possibility that the Hebrew words for strangulation and what happens

19. Hengel, *Crucifixion*, 22.
20. Berrin, *Pesher Nahum Scroll*, 167.

during a crucifixion were associated; however, this was rejected with the Gospels state about Jesus while he showed his disciples proof that it was Jesus standing before them (Luke 24:39), and the nails found during excavations. Although Shani states there is some equivalence between hanging on a tree and the stressing of suffocation or suspension in the Aramaic text, none of these similarities agree with Roman antiquities of the nails as per their custom for a typical crucifixion. It seems unusual that the Romans would change their tactics for one Jewish man and switch to only using ropes, while the other two victims hanging on both sides of Jesus would be nailed.[21]

MINIMAL FACTS

From what is widely accepted by scholars concerning the crucifixion, there are truths that cannot be ignored. In the crucifixion, the first factual thing to be recognized is that the Romans were governing the land during the time of Jesus. The second fact is that the Romans' version of the crucifixion was a horrific event for both Jew or slaves. It was gruesome and bloody. The third fact is that Jesus seen by eyewitnesses being handed over to the Romans to be crucified. These facts are not debatable from a scholarly perspective.

The Quran teaches that Jesus never made it to the cross because God took him (see the previous chapter). The Ahmadiyya Muslims believe that Jesus retreated to India to preach to the lost tribes of Israel. However, these beliefs are not harmonious with other scholars from different backgrounds and their findings. Scholars like Bock, Tacitus, and other Jewish scholars agree that Jesus died on the cross. Therefore, the facts listed here are within reason. If the minimal facts can be agreed upon, then that leaves room for a more conclusive outcome. Since Jesus was handed over to the Romans to be crucified the plausible and more accurate conclusion is that Jesus was executed by the Romans.

21. Harley, "Crucifixion in Roman Antiquity," 309.

Unfortunately, the terms of execution appear to be in question when talking to Muslim members like Deedat. However, since the minimal facts are sound, this means that Jesus went through this tragic ordeal, bloody, hurt, flesh ripped and stabbed. Jesus did not have a blood transfusion or was it recorded that he healed his own injuries. If Deedat would have suggested that Jesus healed his own injuries, then that would present a different view. Instead, stating that the spear in his side revived Jesus, and implicating that one of his disciples tended to Jesus for three days truly means that Jesus was severely injured and incapable of performing a miracle on himself. Furthermore, for that type of severity to have taken place, three days would not be enough time for his disciple to treat his wounds with regular ointments.

Forensic Point of View

While studying the Gospels, the reader cannot truly ascertain the exact cause of death. Could it be the spear to the side, the hardship of the cross, was it the scourging, or could it have been a culmination of all the above? This study has recognized multiple causes for death and believes it to be more advantageous to approach this question from a forensic view. From the above sections, special attention has gone towards pointing out massive blood loss. The Gospels never mentioned that Jesus would cough, have a cold, or have any minor ailment. All is known for a fact is that Jesus would sleep, become hungry, and thirsty.

Luke mentions the sweat becoming blood, but other than that moment, all is uncertain. However, what is certain is that Jesus was beaten, the flesh was ripped, thorns were inserted into his head, and a spear was thrust into his side. In the synopsis, there is a relatively healthy adult male, in his thirties, who would be able to endure some of the punishment, but this punishment was not like the kind one would just walk away from; rather, the punishment Jesus received played a factor in the cause of death. As a person loses blood, the typical response would be disorientation, slow speech, and dehydration. The Gospels tell of his thirst, but Jesus appeared coherent by recognizing his mother, according to John 19:26–27, and Jesus appeared not to be slow of speech when speaking to the other person being crucified as well in Luke 23:41–43. Therefore, blood loss could not be the conclusive decision for the cause of death.

Effects of the Cross

When it concerns a crucifixion, there are several components that highlight its effectiveness. The crucifixion was not meant to be similar to something like beheading or stoning. It was supposed to be long-suffering, humiliating, cruel, and a deterrent for future crimes. None of which foretell how a victim dies, since some were known to perish during the flogging portion. One definition of the crucifixion that this study agrees with was presented by Roger Byard. He defined crucifixion as suspending a victim by his arms from a cross beam until death occurs.[22]

Whether or not the emphasis is Christian terminology or not is irrelevant for this study because the fact remains that Jesus was suspended or hung on the cross and died. The victim would be nailed through the wrists, as the area in the wrist could support the body weight instead of through the hands.[23] The feet were either tied or nailed to the cross so that the legs bend. The victim would occasionally pull themselves up to relieve themselves from the pressure of the weight. However, this would only result in more pain once fatigue settled in and a greater burden on the diaphragm and intercostal muscles as they attempt to maintain respiration.[24] This presents different outcomes for the cause of death, with a strong pull towards asphyxia.

If crucifixion victims suffered from difficulty breathing, agonizing pain from the scourge would add to the said difficulty. However, some scholars are not convinced that Jesus died from

22. Byard, "Forensic and Historical Aspects," 206.
23. Maslen and Piers, "Medical Theories," 187.
24. Byard, "Forensic and Historical Aspects," 207.

asphyxiation. Zugibe was one of those scholars who sought to find the medical justification for Jesus's death and was not convinced that asphyxia was a factor. In his book, *The Crucifixion of Jesus, Completely Revised and Expanded: A Forensic Inquiry,* Zugibe argued that the theory argued by Barbet for asphyxiation was unfounded because he dealt with the *priori* rather than *posteriori,* leading him to focus on a theory that was not archaeological sound.[25] Zugibe's theory was that Jesus died because of internal blood loss due to a fracture.[26] However, this theory does not appear likely due to the emphasis in Scripture stating that his bones were never broken (Ps 34: 20 and John 19:36). Broken bones are mentioned because Zugibe associated fractures with blood loss.

There are other theories associated with the cross that was developed. Theories like pulmonary embolism, broken heart, suspension trauma, hypostudy, and suffocation have all been considered. However, most have been contested by various scholars leaving suffocation and blood loss as more than likely causes of death. The broken heart theory, in the opinion of this study, is a likely contender due to the lack of faith and betrayal of the many who praised Jesus while entering Jerusalem on the donkey, as told in the Gospels. This study will promote that the above theories combined at various levels would attribute to the cause of death because each has proven to be not the absolute answer.

For instance, the theory of suspension trauma was contested by the very nature of crucifixion. "Prolonged immobilization and orthostatic intolerance can occur from the pooling of blood in the lower extremities. There are some cases where an individual would die or faint within an hour of suspension, but since the lower extremities of a crucified person were affixed by nails, the legs were not immobilized or unsupported."[27] Although, with all the facts circling suspension trauma, one cannot deny that this could be a contributing factor while accepting that it was not the sole reason for death. The cross was designed for trauma to occur, to drain the

25. Zugibe, *Crucifixion of Jesus,* 103.

26. Zugibe, *Crucifixion of Jesus,* 135.

27. Bergeron, "Crucifixion of Jesus," 114.

person of energy, and to be the final destination for the execution process, then the grave.

THE OUTCOME OF THE CROSS

As mentioned in the earlier section, the cross was the last place for the person to go before they would be placed in the grave. After the cross, there was no need for more torturing techniques and no need for planning for the next course of punishment. When Jesus was taken down from the cross, he was already pronounced deceased, so the question that the Swoon supporters ask is how. How did Jesus die after being on the cross for such a short amount of time? The medical answer could be found within all the theories.

The first fact, according to the Gospels and other historical documents mentioned in this study, was that Jesus was bleeding and was losing large amounts of blood. The second fact was that Jesus was suspended on the cross for more than an hour, which could contribute to what is known about suspension trauma. The third fact was that being nailed to the cross in the fashion depicted by archaeological findings—nails in the wrists and feet—would cause discomfort in the lungs attributing to some effects of suffocation. The fourth fact was that Jesus was under much stress from being beaten, ridiculed by the people he was sent to save, forced to carry a weighted cross, and other mental strains that could have led to a broken heart.

The fifth medical truth, and assumption, was that Jesus was more than likely in shock from the amount of blood that would have left his body from the scourge, thorns, brutal attack on the head from the soldiers, and the very nails in his wrists. Therefore, it is reasonable to conclude that Jesus died from being suspended, suffering from trauma, lack of breath, and loss of blood. This eliminates the possibility of survival.

6

Conclusion

THROUGHOUT THIS STUDY, SEVERAL goals were kept in mind to help steer the direction of the project. The first mission in mind was seeking to answer the question of whether Jesus could have survived His cross experience. The answer is a resounding, "No!" in the hearts of true believers of Christ (and not just for sentimental reasons). Physically, it was impossible for Jesus to live through the crucifixion and then be resurrected. Still, due to the direction of this study and the charge to share the Gospel with all, the answer differed while considering opinions on the matter from others of different faiths.

It is the hope that upon reading this study, more individuals from different walks of life will come to acknowledge that Jesus of Nazareth died on the cross and ultimately accept the Gospel message that He was raised by God from the dead—thus signifying that Jesus is the promised Savior. The second goal of this study was to help believers explain why Jesus could not have survived the cross from a non-religious and medical perspective. Since some individuals genuinely desire to know about Jesus but have difficulty processing what Scripture states, it should serve as an invaluable guide for those parties before arriving at certain conclusions.

The medical perspective of the crucifixion is not something obscure nor anachronistic. In chapter two, the meta-analysis section, it is mentioned that other scholars have also entertained the thought. Each expert contributed their findings, leaning more toward how they viewed the crucifixion. This study leaned toward a more holistic view that not just one symptom was a factor for Jesus's death. Moreover, it was found throughout this research that not only was the crucifixion engineered to cause difficulty breathing and torture, but the individual would also be in intense pain from the cross and suffering from afflictions such as hemorrhaging and shock.

According to Scripture, Jesus went through the entire process of the crucifixion—meaning that the Romans flogged Jesus with instruments that caused severe physical damage to his body. After that, Jesus had to carry His cross before He was nailed to the cross— information accessible from the Gospels. Furthermore, the Roman execution process was not simple nor easy on the person; it was gruesome, horrendous, bloody, and sad. Although the Roman governor Pilate found "no fault in him" to warrant the crucifixion (Matt 27:24–26), Jesus was still treated as one for whom this form of execution was originally designed.

Muslim scholar Ahmed Deedat (and the whole Ahmadiyya group) believes that Jesus survived the cross. However, there is a contradiction in what is being taught by those who believe Jesus survived. At no point in their argument did they concede nor state that Jesus did not go through the entire process of the crucifixion. Since this is the case, how could he then survive if he was reported dead by the Roman soldier—especially if Jesus was stabbed through the side moments later? Interestingly, in Deedat's work, the stabbing revived Jesus. One critical issue regarding that presumption is that plasma and blood that came out of Jesus, which is an indication of death—not rejuvenation—by medical standards.[1]

Furthermore, if Jesus were to survive the crucifixion after being stabbed in the side and buried in the tomb, he would have

---

1. Bordes, "Clinical Anatomy," 20.

needed to undergo intense, long-term medical care. However, the kind of treatment that Jesus would need to treat his wounds and the hole in his side was not readily available in the era, as the Romans did not offer such services to convicted Jewish prisoners.

Upon acknowledging that Jesus went through these events (according to the Gospels), the next logical question is how Jesus would be able to get out of the tomb. Jesus was battered, and weakened, with no food or drink, and his wounds were still open. Those same wounds would be prone to a serious form of infection while in the tomb. Naturally, Jesus would not have been able to call on the strength to move the boulder from his tomb unless divine intervention was a factor. To add to the difficulty of escaping or having the body stolen, Roman soldiers were posted at the entrance guarding the tomb.

While Deedat believes that Jesus survived the cross, medically, the evidence supports that His death was indeed certain. Jesus was not in any position to simply walk away from the crucifixion without divine intervention. Therefore, if it is accepted that divine intervention was at play, the biblical account logically affirms that God could have raised Jesus from the dead. Also, the fact that divine intervention is a major possibility would refute the idea of Jesus being only a teacher and prophet. For God to step in and raise Jesus from the dead, while all the other prophets in the Bible have died (whether naturally or by the hands of others) states that Jesus was greater than them—a true miracle-worker of epic status.[2]

Furthermore, the conclusion provided by this study is that Jesus died on the cross. He did not survive the ordeal of the crucifixion, and survival was impossible because of the medical factors mentioned in this research. While there are some who will still disagree with this analysis, the logical fact remains that Jesus died on the cross.

The Ahmadiyya camp believes that Jesus was a prophet of God, but Jesus stated that He is the Son of God. If Jesus lied about being the Son, the Christ, then it would be blasphemy, for which

---

2. This study did not participate in the discussion of miracles, but Jesus being raised from the dead constitutes the very definition of a miracle.

God would not have raised Jesus from the dead. However, Jesus was reported dead and was later seen, meaning that Jesus had risen from the dead. God, who is holy and righteous, would not raise someone who was unfairly sharing in glory with him. Jesus stated that he is seated with Father and all authority has been given to him (Luke 22:69 and Col 3:1). Even further, Jesus also stated that he has the authority to forgive sins and that he is the Lord of the Sabbath (Matt 12:8 and Luke 6:5). These are not the words of a prophet of God; rather, these are the words of God, being stated from Jesus Christ, the second person in the Trinity.

Another question answered in this study was why did Jesus have to die? Why did someone who was noted as a teacher, prophet, and good man be subjected to this kind of Roman judgment? The answer is found multiple times in the Old and New Testaments that Jesus Christ had to be sacrificed as a Lamb to save humanity from the sin debt that was incurred from in the very beginning John 1:29 and Hebrews 2:14–18. For Christianity, it means that humanity could not save itself from God's righteous judgment because all have sinned and willfully chosen to remain in their wicked ways, with no escape from the righteous judge. Through a great priest and sacrifice, people can save themselves from God's righteous and holy judgment, but if rejected, how could a righteous and holy God allow sin to go unchecked? Consider what Paul stated in Romans 2:3 and 2 Thessalonians 5–12.

God does not allow rebellion to go unanswered, and he will judge all according to their crimes (Rom 14:10). Therefore, Jesus dying on the cross was necessary to save humanity because he is the Son of God. He, without sin, took on sin to save humanity, according to 2 Corinthians 5:21. Without Christ, mankind would not survive the justice of God, according to Romans 3:21–26.

This study furthers the Christian belief that God raised Jesus from the dead since He was seen later by multiple people and will be seen again in the Second Coming, according to John 14:3, Revelation 1:4–8. The evidence from this research should help those who follow the Quran (and the ideas of Deedat) to understand how the crucifixion worked from a medical perspective. Medically, it was not a regular occurrence for someone to survive the crucifixion without intensive medical treatment, as such was not available for Jesus.

Furthermore, different accounts from separate parties attest to the fact that Jesus was crucified and died. Finally, from all that is presented in this study, many can come to understand the crucifixion from a medical perspective—along with the divine supernatural powers of God and the apologetical understanding of what specifically what happened to Jesus, to help guide them to accept the truth that Jesus Christ is Lord.

The summation of this study from a purely apologetic standpoint is the acceptance of several truths that should be accepted by all. The first truth is that Jesus died on the cross. Jesus dying on the cross destroys the assumption that Jesus was walking around in India or that he somehow hid away while his followers were martyred. Furthermore, it places more severity on the words written in the Gospel during the moment of transfiguration in Matthew 17:5. The undeniable truth behind the cross is salvation.

After the garden, humanity would go on to choose sin over God. It is unavoidable for a person to be sinless. Therefore, atonement must be done; however, as discussed earlier, without a proper sacrifice, without the Lamb of God, humanity had no sustaining means to atone. The Muslim argument suggests that sin is not imputed but instead that their works would help them receive grace from God and, in turn, salvation.

The problem with this theology is that when observing the uniqueness of God, this theology falls apart. God is perfect, which both Christian and Muslim doctrines agree. Naturally, his creation is not perfect, including humanity. Also, man is not perfect and capable of disobeying God. There is no perfect good that humanity can do. So far, both parties should agree with what has been stated. However, since man is not perfect, he will, whether knowingly or unknowingly, sin against a perfect, holy, and righteous God. Being that God is holy and righteous, his judgment must be as well. Furthermore, if someone tried their best to follow the laws given by God, they would fall short, which conclusively means that this individual sinned.

Finally, upon accepting the fact that all other means of atonement pales in comparison to the work of Jesus Christ, the next logical step to agree to with the Gospel doctrine that Jesus was resurrected from the dead. Jesus overcoming death signifies not only what he stated about himself (see Matt 12:40), but also demonstrates that God rose Jesus from the dead—thus paying the sin debt that humanity incurred and causing all of those who believed in Him to live.

Thinking rationally about this, the only one with the power to raise the dead is God. Jesus being raised from the dead means that he was more than just a man, rather something very special. Death should not have authority on a being who is all powerful; yet, death could not hold Jesus. His resurrection not only caused others to believe to in him but fulfilled prophecy concerning a king whose kingdom will never end, as seen in 2 Samuel 7.

Jesus's resurrection proves that God's promises will come to past, and time will not halt those promises. Therefore, the heart of the Muslim theology lacks substance because it suggests that a holy and righteous God will allow sin to be overlooked without sufficient atonement. This book concludes with the quintessential point that humanity needs a perfect savior, one that can advocate for imperfect humanity. Therefore, the crucified Christ is necessary and rational, and Jesus Christ is the only person who could take on this weighty mantle.

Afterword

I OFTEN TEACH MY students to distinguish between essential doctrines of the Christian faith that if denied likely mean the person is not really a Christian and non-essential doctrines that even godly believers disagree on. Few doctrines are as essential as the resurrection. One passage that has been referred to throughout this book is 1 Corinthians 15:14 (NKJV), "And if Christ is not risen, then our preaching is empty and your faith is also empty." Preaching is meaningless without the resurrection. Not only that but forgiveness of sins is impossible without the resurrection as indicated in 1 Corinthians 15:17 (NKJ), "And if Christ is not risen, your faith is futile; you are still in your sins!"

Since this doctrine is so essential to the Christian faith, we should not be surprised that from the moment it happened that Satan had plans in place to dispute whether the resurrection happened. Matthew 28:12–15 records the bribery of the soldiers by the religious leaders to say that the disciples stole Jesus's body. The Swoon Theory is a popular argument against the resurrection and as noted in this book is not only argued by liberal Christian scholars, but atheists, naturalist, Muslim, and Jewish scholars alike. As a result, it is important this argument was addressed as well as it was by Christopher Banks.

Banks does a great job of surveying opposing arguments and refuting them with fairness and charity. His analysis of how different methods of apologetics would address these arguments is also helpful. He also provided medical evidence to show that Jesus would not have survived the crucifixion.

As the academic dean of a Bible college, I enjoy following what our alumni do with their education after leaving our institution. After reading *Did Jesus Survive The Cross?* I can honestly say that Christopher Banks's accomplishment in writing such a great work is among the alumni accomplishments that I am most proud. May God be glorified by this important work!

Joe Parle, Ph.D.
Provost, Academic Dean, and Senior Professor of Bible
College of Biblical Studies, Houston

Bibliography

Abou El Fadl, Khaled. *The Great Theft: Wrestling Islam from the Extremists.* New York: HarperSanFrancisco, 2005.

Anselm, St. *Cur Deus Homo.* London: Forgotten, 2019.

Arrigo, Bruce A., and Carol R. Fowler. "The 'Death Row Community': A Community Psychology Perspective." *Deviant Behavior* 22.1 (2001) 43–71.

Beilby, James. "Varieties of Apologetics." In *Thinking About Christian Apologetics: What It Is and Why We Do It.* Downers Grove: InterVarsity, 2011.

Bergeron, Joseph W. "The Crucifixion of Jesus: Review of Hypothesized Mechanisms of Death and Implications of Shock and Trauma-Induced Coagulopathy." *Journal of Forensic and Legal Medicine* 19.3 (2012) 113–16.

Bernis, Jonathan. *A Rabbi Looks at Jesus of Nazareth.* Grand Rapids: Chosen, 2011.

Berrin, Shani L. *The Pesher Nahum Scroll from Qumran an Exegetical Study of 4Q169.* Leiden: Brill, 2004.

Bhattacharya, Subham, Mrinal Kanti Das, Suman Sarkar, and Avishek De. "Hematidrosis." *Indian Pediatrics* 50.7 (2013) 703–4.

Blomberg, Craig. *Matthew (Vol. 22). The New American Commentary.* Nashville: Broadman & Holman, 1992.

Bordes, Stephen et al. "The Clinical Anatomy of Crucifixion." *Clinical Anatomy* 33.1 (2020) 12–21.

Broderick, Stephen R., and Stephen R. Broderick. "Hemothorax." *Thoracic Surgery Clinics* 23.1 (2013) 89–96.

Burhani, Ahmad Najib. "The Ahmadiyya and the Study of Comparative Religion in Indonesia: Controversies and Influences." *Islam & Christian Muslim Relations* 25.2 (2014) 141–58.

Byard, Roger W. "Forensic and Historical Aspects of Crucifixion." *Forensic Science, Medicine and Pathology* 12.2 (2016) 206–8.

Chapman, David W. *Ancient Jewish and Christian Perceptions of Crucifixion.* Tübingen: Mohr Siebeck, 2008.

Cilliers, L., and François P. Retief. "The History and Pathology of Crucifixion: History of Medicine." *South African Medical Journal* 93.12 (2003) 938–41.

Craig, William Lane. "Was Jesus Buried in Shame? Reflections on B. McCane's Proposal." *Expository Times* 115.12 (2004) 404–9.

Crawford, Sidnie White. *Scribes and Scrolls at Qumran*. Grand Rapids: William B. Eerdmans, 2019.

Dal Bo, Federico. "Jesus' Trial in the Latin Talmud." *Henoch* 41.1 (2019) 140–76.

De Caro, Liberato, and Cinzia Giannini. "Turin Shroud Hands' Region Analysis Reveals the Scrotum and a Part of the Right Thumb." *Journal of Cultural Heritage* 24 (2017) 140–46.

DeBoer, Scott. "A Trauma Patient Unlike Any Other: A Medical Review of the Crucifixion." *Australasian Emergency Nursing Journal* 10.4 (2007) 217.

Deedat, Ahmed. *Crucifixion or Cruci-Fiction; Resurrection or Resuscitation: The God That Never Was*. Montreal: Dar El-Ulum Foundation, 1993.

Eisenberg, Leonard Irwin. "A New Natural Interpretation of the Empty Tomb." *International Journal for Philosophy of Religion* 80.2 (2016) 133–43.

Embrayil, Mathew. *Jesus' Life in India: A Search for the Truth*. Hamburg: Tredition Verlag, 2017.

Geivett, Douglas, and Gary Habermas. *In Defense of Miracles: A Comprehensive Case for God's Action in History*. Downers Grove: InterVarsity, 1997.

Geyser-Fouché, Ananda. "Crucifixion at Qumran." *Hervormde Teologiese Studies* 70.1 (2014) 1–12.

Goldin, Hyman E. *Hebrew Criminal Law and Procedure*. Broadway: Twayne, 1952.

Habermas, Gary, et al. "Medical Views on the Death by Crucifixion of Jesus Christ." *Proceedings* 34.6 (2021) 748–52.

Habermas, Gary R. "Q&A: Naturalistic Theories." In *LBTS Faculty Publications and Presentations*. Lynchburg: Liberty University, 2010.

Habermas, Gary R., and Michael R. Licona. *The Case for the Resurrection of Jesus*. Grand Rapids: Kregel, 2004.

Harley, Felicity. "Crucifixion in Roman Antiquity: The State of the Field." *Journal of Early Christian Studies* 27.2 (2019) 303–23.

Hengel, Martin. *Crucifixion: In the Ancient World and the Folly of the Message of the Cross*. Minneapolis: 1517 Media, 2003.

Hengel, Martin, Anna Maria, Wayne Schwemer, Coppins, and Simon Gathercole. *Jesus and Judaism*. Waco: Baylor University Press, 2019.

Hoffman, Marie T. "Incarnation, Crucifixion, and Resurrection in Psychoanalytic Thought." *Journal of Psychology and Christianity* 29.2 (2010) 121.

Holmén, Tom. "Crucifixion Hermeneutics in Judaism at the Time of Jesus." *Journal for the Study of the Historical Jesus* 14.3 (2016) 197–222.

Huss, Brian. "Cultural Differences and the Law of Noncontradiction: Some Criteria for Further Research." *Philosophical Psychology* 17.3 (2004) 375–89.

Joseph, Simon J. "Jesus in India? Transgressing Social and Religious Boundaries." *Journal of the American Academy of Religion* 80.1 (2012) 161–99.

Khouri, Sherene Nicholas. "The Crucifixion in the Qur'an: Answering Muslim's Claims Regarding the Death of Jesus Christ." *Transformation* 38.2 (2021) 158–74.

Kraemer, David Charles. *A History of the Talmud.* Cambridge: Cambridge University Press, 2019.

Komoszewski, J. Ed, et al. *Reinventing Jesus: How Contemporary Skeptics Miss the Real Jesus and Mislead Popular Culture.* Grand Rapids: Kregel, 2006.

Lawson, Todd. *The Crucifixion and the Qur'an: A Study in the History of Muslim Thought.* New York City: Simon and Schuster, 2014.

Lee, Michael E. "Historical Crucifixion: A Liberationist Response to Deep Incarnation." *Theological Studies* 81.4 (2020) 892–912.

Lutzer, Erwin. *Slandering Jesus: Six Lies People Tell About the Man Who Said He Was God.* Carol Stream: Tyndale House, 2007.

Marotti, Jonathan D., and Edward J. Gutmann. "Hemosiderin-laden Mesothelial Cells in a Pericardial Effusion." *Diagnostic Cytopathology* 47.9 (2019) 963–65.

Maslen, Matthew W., and Piers D. Mitchell. "Medical Theories on the Cause of Death in Crucifixion." *Journal of the Royal Society of Medicine* 99.4 (2006) 185–8.

Matsuoka, Ryo, and Manabu Tanaka. "Hematidrosis in a Japanese Girl: Treatment with Propranolol and Psychotherapy." *Pediatrics International* 62.8 (2020) 1001–2.

McBrien, Richard. "Disobedience Can Crucify One, Then or Now (New Testament)." *National Catholic Reporter* 29.44 (1993) 2.

McDowell, Josh., and John Gilchrist. *The Islam Debate.* San Bernardino: Campus Crusade for Christ, 1983.

Mitchell, Piers D. "Improving the Use of Historical Written Sources in Paleopathology." *International Journal of Paleopathology* 19 (2017) 88–95.

Morgan, Garry R. *Understanding World Religions in 15 Minutes.* Bloomington: Bethany House, 2012.

Newman, H. I. "The Death of Jesus in the Toledot Yeshu Literature." *Journal of Theological Studies* 50.1 (1999) 59–79.

Nicolotti, Andrea. "The Scourge of Jesus and the Roman Scourge." *Journal for the Study of the Historical Jesus* 15.1 (2017) 1–59.

Ohlow, Marc-Alexander, Bernward Lauer, Michele Brunelli, and J. Christoph Geller. "Incidence and Predictors of Pericardial Effusion After Permanent Heart Rhythm Device Implantation: Prospective Evaluation of 968 Consecutive Patients." *Circulation Journal: Official Journal of the Japanese Circulation Society* 77.4 (2013) 975–81.

Parrott, Justin. "Jesus: A Foundation for Dialogue Between Muslims and Christians." *Yaqeen Institute for Islamic Research* (2018). https://yaqeeninstitute.org/justin-parrott/jesus-a-foundation-for-dialogue-between-muslims-and-christians/

Pierson, Richard N., Lars Burdorf, Joren C. Madsen, Gregory D. Lewis, and David A. D'Alessandro. "Pig-to-human Heart Transplantation: Who Goes First?" *American Journal of Transplantation* 20.10 (2020) 2669–74.

Regan, Jacqueline M., Kiarash Shahlaie, and Joseph C. Watson. "Crucifixion and Median Neuropathy." *Brain and Behavior* 3.3 (2013) 243–48.

Reynolds, Gabriel Said. "The Muslim Jesus: Dead or Alive?" *Bulletin of the School of Oriental and African Studies* 72.2 (2009) 237–58.

Sadouni, Samadia. "Ahmed Deedat, Internationalisation, and Transformations of Islamic Polemic." *Journal of Religion in Africa* 43.1 (2013) 53–73.

Salahi, M. A. *The Qur'an: A Translation for the 21st Century.* Leicestershire: The Islamic Foundation, 2019.

Shamoun, Sam. "The Crucifixion of Christ: A Fact, Not Fiction." *Journal of Biblical Apologetics* 8 (2003) 52–64.

Smith, Graeme. *Was the Tomb Empty?: A Lawyer Weighs the Evidence for the Resurrection.* Chicago: Lion Hudson, 2014.

Smith, Mark D. *The Final Days of Jesus: The Thrill of Defeat, The Agony of Victory: A Classical Historian Explores Jesus's Arrest, Trial, and Execution.* Cambridge: Lutterworth, 2018.

Smither, Edward L., and Trevor Castor. "Timothy I of Baghdad: A Model for Peaceful Dialogue." In *The History of Apologetics.* Benjamin K. Forrest, Joshua D. Chatraw, and Alister E. McGrath, eds. Grand Rapids: Zondervan Academic, 2020.

Stroud, William. *A Treatise on the Physical Cause of the Death of Christ.* Hamilton and Adams, 1847.

Sumner, Darren O. "Jesus and the God of Israel: God Crucified and Other Studies on the New Testament's Christology of Divine Identity—By Richard Bauckham, William B. Eerdmans." *Reviews in Religion and Theology* 17.2 (2010) 125–27.

Twelftree, Graham H. "Jesus, Magician or Miracle Worker." *The Biblical Annals* 10 (2020): 405–36.

Vidu, Adonis. *Atonement, Law, and Justice: The Cross in Historical and Cultural Contexts.* Grand Rapids: Baker Academic, 2014.

Wang, Zhaoyue, et al. "A Case of Hematidrosis Successfully Treated with Propranolol." *American Journal of Clinical Dermatology* 11.6 (2010) 440–43.

Zafar, Harris. *Demystifying Islam: Tackling the Tough Questions.* Lanham: Rowman & Littlefield, 2014.

Zeitlin, Solomon. "The Crucifixion of Jesus Re-Examined." *The Jewish Quarterly Review* 31.4 (1941) 327–69.

Zugibe, Frederick T. *The Crucifixion of Jesus, Completely Revised and Expanded: A Forensic Inquiry.* New York: M. Evans, 2005.

———. *The Crucifixion of Jesus a Forensic Inquiry.* New York: Evans, 2005.

Subject Index

Ahmadiyya, 14, 15, 23, 55, 56, 68, 75, 81

Ally, Shabir, 15, 18

St. Anselm, 35, 36, 37

Antiquities, 29, 68

Apologetics, 7, 33, 39, 41, 43, 56, 58

Apostle Paul, 1, 3, 24, 25, 45, 60

Archaeological, 6, 10, 29, 71, 72

Asphyxiation, 9, 10, 11, 52, 62, 71

Atonement, x, 35, 37, 50, 78, 84

Balaam, 21, 22

Beilby, James, 40

Blood Loss, xi, 10, 62, 67, 69, 70, 71

Burial, 25, 31, 32

Cardiac Rupture, 28

Christian, xi, 1, 3, 4, 6, 16, 24, 35

Christology 36, 84

Cosmological Argument 37, 39

Craig, William Lane, 25, 58

Cross, x, 2, 4, 5, 7, 12, 14, 18, 24, 31, 49

Crucifixion, xi, 8, 9, 10, 11, 13, 23, 27, 28, 31, 33, 45

Crux, 11, 18

Deedat, Ahmed, 2, 3, 5, 13, 14, 54

Designer Argument, 37, 39

Ehrman, Bart, 6

Essenes, 19, 20

Flagellation, 66

Flogging, 10, 29, 56, 65, 70

Forensic, 9, 28, 29, 63, 64, 69, 70, 71, 80

God, x, xiii, 1, 2, 3, 4, 15, 16, 17, 25, 30, 34, 35, 36, 39

Gospels, xii, 3, 4, 5, 6, 15, 17, 19, 21, 24, 29

Habermas, Gary, 7, 9, 18, 24, 41, 43, 50, 58, 61, 66

Harris, Zafar, 9, 15, 55

Hemothorax, 52, 62, 63, 81

Hematidrosis, 64, 65

Hermeneutical, 4, 5, 42

Hume, David, 26, 27

Hypovolemic Shock, 28

Josephus, 19, 20, 21, 24

Judaism, 1, 18, 22, 82

Messianic Jews, 22

Muslim, 5, 6, 8, 9, 13, 15, 16, 17, 23

Pericardium, 28

Pharisees, 19, 20, 21

Presupposition, 39, 40, 41, 42, 43, 58

Prophet, x, xii, 2, 6, 14, 15, 16, 18, 25, 29, 30, 38, 48, 51

Quran, 2, 12, 15, 17, 18, 21, 48, 56, 59, 68

Resurrection, x, 2, 3, 6, 13, 16, 19, 20
Romans, 2, 8, 20, 26, 23, 24, 35, 45, 48, 49, 50, 61, 66, 76
Ruptured Heart, 10, 28

Sadducees, 19, 20
Sanhedrin, 20, 21, 22, 26
Savior, xiv, 1, 14, 22, 33, 35, 36, 42, 47, 60, 73, 78
Schäfer, Peter, 21, 45
Shock, 10, 12, 28, 72, 74, 81

Shroud of Turin, 30
Sproul, R. C., 34, 35, 36, 38
Swoon Theory, xi, iv, iii, 3, 14, 16, 18, 28, 55, 56, 79

Tacitus, 18, 24, 66, 68
Talmud, 19, 20, 21, 45, 82
Tanakh, 19
Teleological Argument, 39
Thoracic, 62, 63, 81
Torah, 19, 21
Trauma, xi, 2, 9, 10, 12, 28, 49, 51, 56, 62, 71, 72, 82

Zeitlin, Solomon, 19, 20, 84
Zugibe, Frederick, 9, 10, 11, 28, 70, 71, 84